MISSION POSSIBLE

MISSION POSSIBLE

Becoming a World-Class Organization While There's Still Time

KEN BLANCHARD

&

TERRY WAGHORN

WITH JIM BALLARD

McGraw-Hill

NEW YORK   SAN FRANCISCO   WASHINGTON, D.C.   AUCKLAND   BOGOTÁ

CARACAS   LISBON   LONDON   MADRID   MEXICO CITY   MILAN

MONTREAL   NEW DELHI   SAN JUAN   SINGAPORE

SYDNEY   TOKYO   TORONTO

Library of Congress catalog card number: 96-77499

McGraw-Hill

A Division of The McGraw-Hill Companies

Copyright © 1997 by Blanchard Management Corporation and Terry Waghorn. All rights reserved. Printed in the United States of America. Except as permitted under the United States Copyright Act of 1976, no part of this publication may be reproduced or distributed in any form or by any means, or stored in a data base or retrieval system, without the prior written permission of the publisher.

4 5 6 7 8 9 0   D O C / D O C   9 0 1 0 9 8 7

ISBN 0-07-005940-3

Book design by Michael Mendelsohn.

McGraw-Hill books are available at special quantity discounts to use as premiums and sales promotions, or for use in corporate training programs. For more information, please write to the Director of Special Sales, McGraw-Hill, 11 West 19th Street, New York, NY 10011. Or contact your local bookstore.

This book is printed on recycled, acid-free paper containing a minimum of 50% recycled, de-inked fiber.

To everyone living in organizations today
who are dealing with the reality of having
to improve their present operation and
design their future at the same time

CONTENTS

FOREWORD

This is a book about hope. Rather than serving up yet another rendition of the difficulties currently besetting our nations and corporations, Ken and Terry's book takes us on a path of growth and renewal. They show us, in very convincing terms, that there is a light at the end of the tunnel, and that by embracing a few simple truths, we can all start moving towards it.

At the center of their argument is the need for today's companies to establish and maintain a healthy balance between continuity and innovation. Concentrating on the present with scant regard for the future is akin to driving forward while looking out the rear-view mirror. Eventually you're destined to hit something. Similarly, overinvesting in tomorrow's opportunities without first protecting and shoring up your current businesses can be disastrous—you're likely to run out of steam before tomorrow arrives. Getting to the future first is essentially a two-step process: improving the present while creating the future. Neither step takes precedence over the other. Both are critical.

Self-evident as this argument may be, the fact is that it's seldom applied in practice. Many leaders like to believe they keep things in balance, but in reality most put much more energy into preserving what they have than creating that which they don't have. Present pressures always seem to win out over future considerations. Thus, most organizational transformation agendas are more about improving the present than they are about creating the future. As yesteryear's "mass" markets continue to decompose into ever smaller market niches, it is becoming increasingly apparent that tomorrow's market leaders will be those who are able to continually differentiate themselves. Costs, quality, and speed will become prerequisites for survival. Success will become increasingly tied to innovation and creativity. Rather than looking at their markets through a single lens, managers must begin looking at them through bifocal lenses—they must become skilled at scanning the horizon for new opportunities, while keeping their eyes on the road they are presently on.

Difficult as it may be, developing bifocal vision is only one of the challenges facing today's leaders. Another is the need to find a balance between the opposing interests of the company's different stakeholders. Shareholders seek a quick return on their investment, employees want security and increased benefits, and customers want your product or service to be high quality but low price. Trying to keep everyone happy at all times is impossible. It's a matter of sustaining a healthy tension between the different constituencies, taking care never to let things get skewed too far in any one direction. This is not easily accomplished, yet by recognizing the pressures built into the system, by using information technology to build bridges and destroy walls, and by building a sense of community around a shared vision and set of values, trust between these different stakeholders can flourish and all things become possible.

This is what Ken and Terry's book is all about. Read it once, then put it aside for awhile and let your thoughts ferment. Then read it again, and let it do its magic on you. We think you will find it worth the investment of your time. As its simple truths begin to penetrate your soul you'll come to discover that it really is true—everything is possible.

We wish you success on your journey.

Jon Madonna
Chairman
KPMG International

Ruud Koedijk
Member, Executive Committee KPMG
Chairman, KPMG Europe

ACKNOWLEDGMENTS

The book you are holding is the result of a unique partnership between two very different people. Ken has spent most of his career discussing and writing about management's so-called soft S's (staff, skills, styles, and shared values). Terry has focused his career energy almost exclusively on the hard S's (strategy, structure, and systems). Yet, holding true to the adage that opposites attract, we quickly came to discover that our differences could actually be a blessing in disguise. One of us was strong where the other was weak, and vice versa. As this realization became more apparent, our relationship strengthened and a friendship was born. This book is a by-product of that friendship.

There is an invisible corps of people who have contributed greatly to this book's development that we want to thank.

First and foremost is our writing partner and spiritual guide *Jim Ballard* for his tireless energy, creativity, and commitment to this project. Once Terry did the initial draft, Ken and Jim worked almost nonstop together to produce the next draft. From that point on we worked closely together on further drafts. You're the best, Jim! Thanks for being there for us and bringing the spiritual energy of the Big Five.

Richard Narramore, our McGraw-Hill editor, for being

instrumental in helping us set the rhythm and flow of the book.

Margret McBride, our literary agent for believing in the project and helping us to get the best possible publisher.

BTD and *KPMG* our respective "corporate sponsors" for supporting the years of thinking and research that went into the writing of this book and for our colleagues always being there when we needed them. Eight people, in particular, are worthy of mention for their stoic support, helpful feedback, and enduring patience: *Margie Blanchard*, *Pete Psichogios*, and *Dale Truax* from *BTD*, and *Ruud Koedijk*, *Wessel Ganzevoort*, *Suzanne Maxwel*, *Steven Olthof*, and *Paul Woudstra* from *KPMG*.

We also want to acknowledge *Eleanor Terndrup* and *Michele Jansen* for their patient and skillful typing of the final manuscript and *David Witt* for his help on the references and bibliography. *BTD* is lucky to have them on its team.

Much of the wisdom found within the pages of this book came from the words or works of others, be they management theorists, ancient philosophers, or contemporary practitioners. All those cited in the book have been recognized in the references and bibliography at the end of the book. It is a small token of appreciation for the influence they have had on our work. We do want to single out *Ichak Adizes*, *Gerry Faust*, *Mary Gelinas*, *Gene Hall*, *Gary Hamel*, *Charles Handy*, *Roger James*, *C. K. Prahalad*, *Michael Treacy*, *Fred Wiersma*, *Drea Zigarmi*, and *Patricia Zigarmi* for special mention. Their work rose to the top as we wrote this book.

Writing is something that is very personal, and as such can be a lonely business. Each thought takes time to nurture and develop, and can become so all consuming that other aspects of life are temporarily put on the back burner. Quite naturally, that can make life somewhat difficult for family members and close friends. However, in our case, both of us had relations that were up to the challenge. To *Margie* and *Martine* go our love and thanks. From *Jim Ballard* goes the same to *Barbara Perman*. To *Dorothy, Scott,* and *Debbie Blanchard, Margaret* and *Gerald Waghorn, Philippe Naert, Daniel DeVeusser, Walter Blomme* and *Luk Grosemans* go our gratitude and appreciation.

INTRODUCTION

It is possible that most people working after the turn of the century will be working in industries that don't even exist now.

Nicholas Imparto and Oren Harari, **Jumping the Curve**

Once there was a time in business when you could experience a change and then return to a period of relative stability. That era was followed by one in which, as soon as you got one change handled, you had to get ready for another.

Nowaways, the changes are occurring rapid fire—one on top of another. There's no rest and there's no getting ready. In the heat of this chaos, it's hard for people to maintain perspective. This situation reminds us of the story about the little girl who comes home from school one day and asks her mother (today it certainly could be her father), "Why does Daddy work so late every night?" The mother, in an understanding way, replies, "Well, honey, Daddy just doesn't have time to finish all his work during the day." The little girl, in her infant wisdom, says, "Then why don't they put him in a slower group?"

Alas, there are no slower groups. Constant change is a way

of life in business. In fact, to stay competitive today, you not only have to pay attention to what you're doing now in order to perform better, but to what you have to do tomorrow to stay competitive in the future. In other words, you have to simultaneously manage the present and plan the future. To highlight this idea, we ask you to consider the following metaphor.

ON THE BEACH

Visualize a large sandcastle that has been built at the edge of the water. Several features of the sandcastle are suggestive of the traditional organization: its roughly pyramidal shape, its rising turrets, the crusted wall and battlements. The group of people who built this castle have until recently been working to improve it: rechanneling the moat, shoring up the main entrance, rebuilding the wall by using sticks for reinforcements, etc. Now the tide has come in, and parts of the castle have been eaten away by the invading waters. Having seen what high tide has done to other castles, the group realizes that efforts to rebuild the old castle have been for naught. As the rising waves continue to bite into the foundation, the group concludes it's only a matter of time before its structure will cease to exist, so the group gives up and wanders off disconsolately down the beach.

Now also imagine that at the upper end of this castle, above the tide line, a newer, flatter structure is being formed by a second group. The group working on this project is sculpting a flat, streamlined structure, a more efficient version of the old castle, precisely at the tide line. This group's notion is that by building its structure above the point the waters can reach, and by making it flat and aerodynamic, the model will be safe from wind and wave.

On a bluff overlooking the beach, above the activity of the waves altogether, stands a third group of people. Eyes are on the horizon as people glimpse an approaching storm. To this group it's clear that the storm will wipe out not only the remains of the original castle but the improved structure built by the second group as well. This third group is intent on fashioning a whole new way of operating that is nomadic in nature. It is not interested in building a permanent structure, as the other groups wanted to do. Instead it dreams of being able to break camp almost instantaneously in order to pounce upon emerging opportunities, regardless of the changing environmental conditions it faces.

The three groups in the sandcastle metaphor represent three distinct kinds of responses that organizations are making to the need for change today.

1. The first group sees no need to change. Its members believe that whatever got them to where they are today will suffice to get

them through tomorrow. In the spirit of Scarlett O'Hara in *Gone With the Wind*, they say, "I'll think about it tomorrow." They are frozen in time, paralyzed at the prospect of changing the status quo. Because of this they are no longer in tune with their markets, and thus no match for their more fleet-footed competitors. The future for them looks bleak.

2. The second group is not fixated on yesterday's success formula, and its members recognize the need to constantly improve what they already have. They are striving to fortify their present ways of operating in an effort to build and sustain customer loyalties in current served markets.

3. The third group is focused on the future, committed to creating new competitive arenas. Its members recognize that even if they get better, they can still be put out of business by an unexpected change in markets, customer needs, or technology. Realizing that tomorrow's customers are unlikely to resemble those of today, they are busy dreaming about and creating what could be.

With the first group out of the race we're left with the last two, which brings us to this important inquiry:

QUESTION

Which approach
is better—

improving
what is,

or

creating
what isn't?

ANSWER

Yes!

In other words, do both. Why? For the simple reason that focusing on either dimension while ignoring the other is a formula for failure. If you don't organize your company to make decisions faster and to move closer to the customer, you're likely to lose the market to a quicker competitor. However, if your fascination with what you already have precludes you from creating what you don't have, you're likely to end up as an accident on the highway to the future. A balance must be struck between continuity and innovation. You can't have one without the other, both are essential. *Al Dunlap*, former Chairman and CEO of *Scott Paper Company*, has said it well:

> There are three types of executives in the world. There are those who can get short-term results and haven't a clue where they're going to take the company in the future. Conversely, there are those who have a great ten-year plan but are going to be out of business in ten months. And then there are those who can get short-term results in conjunction with a vision for the future. These are the good ones. But they are in unbelievably short supply.

It's always been hard to do two things well at the same time. How can you do a good job of managing the present when you're worried about the future? How can you effectively scan the horizon of the future when you're concerned about the present?

To appreciate the difficulty of striking a balance between these two important objects of attention consider the words of

F. Scott Fitzgerald: "The test of a first-rate intelligence is the ability to hold two conflicting ideas in mind at the same time, and still retain the ability to function." ***Getting people to break out of their current world view while continuing to operate within it*** is difficult even for the best of us. Yet in today's hyper-competitive markets, it must be done. We have no choice. We must work on the present and the future at the same time. As *Steve Case*, CEO of *America On Line*, said when he was asked if he was currently focusing more on *AOL's* daily operations, or on its place in cyberspace, "Right now I'm kind of doing both. We're looking to hire a chief operating officer to handle more of the day-to-day details, but until then I'm doing both."

The purpose of this book is to help you develop your capacity to do exactly that—manage the present effectively while at the same time creating the future. The book is designed to be a thought-provoker rather than a how-to-manual. Since your present and future realities will be unique to your own particular set of circumstances, our goal is not to define them for you. Instead we will provide you with some concepts, ideas, and frameworks that can help you on your journey toward world class status.

We've divided the book into five chapters:

1. Once Upon a Sandcastle: Building Tomorrow Today
2. Redesigning the Castle: First-Curve Improvements
3. Taking the High Ground: Second-Curve Innovations

4. Putting the Right People on the Right Team with the Right Kind of Support

5. Do I Have What It Takes to Live in a Two-Curve World?

The first three chapters build on our sandcastle analogy. Chapter 1 presents our rationale for why working simultaneously on both the present (improving the existing castle) and the future (fashioning an entirely new kind of living arrangement) is so important. Chapter 2 contains our best thinking on improving your present operation, and in Chapter 3 we address the second critical focus, creating the future. In Chapter 4 we discuss who should be doing what and examine how to harmonize differing personality styles so as to ensure that desired improvements are implemented and future innovations receive the necessary support from both management and employees. The focus of the final chapter is personal, contending that the journey toward world-class status and the necessary changes to achieve it begin *within* people, whether they are leaders, managers, or individual contributors. We invite you now to set out on that journey with us.

Ken Blanchard
Terry Waghorn

MISSION POSSIBLE

CHAPTER ONE

ONCE UPON A SANDCASTLE: BUILDING TOMORROW TODAY

The significant problems we face cannot be solved at the same level at which we created them.

Albert Einstein

Pretty much everyone agrees that in order to succeed today, organizations must be fast and flexible and continuously improving. Leaders are finding out, however, that it's by no means easy to get people committed to constant change. They may understand that change is required and know precisely what it is that must be changed. They may even want it to happen. Nevertheless, human nature tends to want to hold on to old ways of doing things. People often are stuck in the thinking that got them to where they are today, even though that thinking can't be used to get them where they need to be tomorrow.

We think there's a way out of this mess. It is based on three key points:

1. Success in organizations is all about creative use of untapped human energy.
2. The way to tap this energy is to make people your partners.
3. The way to make people your partners is to meaningfully engage them in either improving the present operation of the organization or creating its future.

FOCUSING AND DIRECTING HUMAN ENERGY

Marvin Weisbord, author of **Productive Workplaces,** was talking about the need to transcend the past when he wrote: "If I could ask one thing of a crystal ball in every new situation, it would not be, 'What's wrong and what will fix it?' It would be, 'What's possible here, and who cares?'" Wouldn't it be wonderful if all the people in an organization could ask this question as they considered together their future? Somehow that organization would have found a way to gather the creative energies of its people and focus their efforts far beyond business-as-usual thinking.

Human energy is like the energy of light. When it is dissipated, as in the average light bulb, it gets work done in an average way. But when that same energy is focused and concentrated in a single direction, as with a laser beam, it has the power to cut through any kind of obstacle. In the same way, whereas the average person disperses his/her energy into a broad spectrum of pursuits, the person of "genius" is able to harness his or her energy, beam it toward one single pursuit at a time, and accomplish far more than others. This principle of concentration of energy also applies when you are considering the efforts of a large group of people—an organization. The success of that organization is directly related to the amount of energy its people are willing to invest, and to its ability to harness and direct those energies toward a single, burning purpose.

FREEING UP BRAIN POWER

Most of us have no idea what we can produce in a given span of time, until we're called upon to do so. We're operating at a fraction of the energy and brain power available to us, and we don't even know it. Then something comes into our experience that focuses our attention and engages our mind. We start to look at the world through new eyes. For example, suppose you've never owned a red car—never even thought of owning one. But one day you go out to shop for a new car and lo and behold, you drive home a brand-new fire-engine-red automobile! Now, whenever you're out in traffic, which cars do you think you'll be noticing? The red ones—they seem to be everywhere! They were there all along, you just weren't noticing them.

In the same way, when you're engaged in an ongoing project—a hobby, a work project, or something you're writing or building—you find your mind consumed by it. Wherever you are—at the store, driving your car, reading a magazine—your attention gravitates to objects, people, and events that have a connection to your project. Whatever you see, whatever you're doing, becomes related to it. When this happens to you we say you are engaged in **project consciousness.**

Suppose an organization could find a way to organize and engage its people's attention around the purpose of making the organization significantly better. Suppose this people's collective imagination were triggered, to the extent that the improvement agenda became not just a goal but a mission. Suppose a way were found for each person to experience ownership of and responsibility for a specific "patch" of the collective "quilt" and encouraged to use his or her discretionary time for working on that particular piece of the action. **This would become a setup for project consciousness to kick in.** As that person looked out at the world through the framework of his or her improvement project, everything he or she saw would become

4

a potentially rich resource for doing creative work on the project assignment. By harnessing the creative potential of all its people's project consciousness, the organization could "beam" their efforts so as to produce results far beyond what would have been thought possible.

PARTNERING FOR THE FUTURE

Once you have understood and appreciated this principle of the concentration of energy, as it's applied to a whole organization of people, the next question you must ponder is, "How do I tap that energy to transform my organization?" The answer is to make people partners and involve them directly in decision making. Marvin Weisbord again: "The quickest way to increase dignity, meaning, and community in a workplace is to involve people in redesigning their work. That is also the shortest route—in the long run—to lower cost, higher quality, and more satisfied customers."

We think the only way leaders and working people can effectively enter the future is as partners. People who work must become full participants in the process of determining how their working conditions and the nature of their tasks can be improved in the short run (the present) and the long run (the future). How do you create this partnership between the leadership and the work force in your organization? One elegant way is through the power of human choice. It's been well established that when a radically innovative idea is proposed to the mind, the mind's first tendency is to ask how it could be made real. Since the mind is using old thinking as it ponders this question, it can't see its way to the finished product, so it rejects the idea out of hand. The mind reacts differently, however, when it is asked to choose between two or more alternatives. The energy of attention then is directed not to **yes** or **no** but to **which**. To illustrate this principle, we ask you to imagine yourself in the following scenario.

You are in a final interview for a new job. Your would-be department manager opens your meeting by saying, "From our perspective, we'd be very happy to have you join our team. Since you're here today, I assume that decision is mutual. But before finalizing our relationship I'd like to cover one more important aspect of your job."

Then the manager smiles, leans forward, and says, "We've learned over the years that most people in the world of work have more creative energy and brain power than they use on the job. If we can tap into and focus some of this discretionary energy on improving our present operation or designing our future, the payoff can be tremendous. Consequently, we say that everyone in our organization has two jobs. One is his or her 'day job'—in some way helping to provide customers with high quality products and services. Second, each person has a 'transformation job.' In this capacity you'd be playing on one of two teams. If you join our company, we want to offer you a choice of which of those two teams you wish to join.

"The first team we call a 'P Team.' The P stands for present. A P Team has the job of revising our present organization so that we can be more responsive to our customers today. Its focus is on improvement. The second team is an 'F Team.' The F stands for future. The task of an F Team is to create the future by imagining what customers and markets will be like then. Its focus is on innovation. Both teams operate at the same time. We see the work of these two teams as being the only way we can achieve our goal of becoming a world-class organization. You can help us to do that."

As you're pondering all of this, the manager hands you a card and says, "To help you decide which team you want to play on, read over this list of questions and see what you think."

FOCUS QUESTIONS

- Which has more appeal for you—improving what is or creating what isn't?

- Do you see yourself as more of a maintenance engineer or an architect?

- Are you more interested in doing things right or doing the right things?

- Would you prefer to tune a carburetor or build a rocket ship?

- Would you rather implement a direction or determine it?

- Would you rather produce results now or design how they'll be produced in the future?

The manager goes on to say, "If you prefer the first choice in each question, you would probably want to join a P Team, but if the second choice is more enticing, membership on an F Team might be more attractive. Both teams are vital to our organization. You can only be on one team, though, so take some time to think it over. If you decide to join us, I'll need your answer within a few days. You see, every other Friday afternoon all over the organization for an hour and a half, P Team and F Team meetings of six to ten people are taking place. That's where everyone brings what they've observed and learned during the last two weeks about improvement (if they're on a P Team) or innovation (if they're on an F Team). Each team is a means of information gathering and collating. Collectively they are the eyes and ears of this organization. The whole purpose of this plan is to make practical use of the brain power of every person to move the organization forward. It's an exciting partnership process."

"How does the work of all these teams get coordinated and supported?" you ask.

"Good question. Two organization-wide design teams make the partnership process work," the manager replies. "The work of these design teams is critical, because they deal with organization-wide issues that cross department lines. One design team coordinates the work of all the P Teams; the other the work of the F Teams. Members of these two design teams (both managerial and nonmanagerial) have been nominated by employees. Each design team has two functions: to be a clearinghouse of information and a coordinator of projects. The design teams make sure that the best ideas generated by their respective P and F Teams are implemented. Often that involves asking P and F Teams to work on certain implementation projects. Overseeing the work of these design teams is a steering committee made up of the top management of the organization. Their main responsibility is to maintain the proper balance between improving the present and designing the future.

"So that's the story", the manager concludes, "It's been a pleasure talking with you and we'll talk again in a couple of days."

What we've described here is a plan for eliciting the creative energy now lying dormant in people in all parts of an organization. Companies that flourish in the coming decades will be those that devise a plan for not just eliciting but also marshaling that energy.

It should be clear from our discussion that an organization can profit immensely through the utilization of:

1. ***The concentration of people's energy,*** applied in the form of project consciousness to the process of organizational change.
2. ***The power of choice*** used as a strategy to get people to commit to the change process (as opposed to just handing them a plan they can say "yes" or "no" to).
3. ***Partnering,*** by engaging people's natural desire to improve or create the way they do their work.

When we put these ideas together we have the makings of the major concept of this book: ***working on the present and the future of your organization at the same time.*** We think this can be done without creating schizoid executives, by assigning the tasks of present and future focus to different groups of people.

RIDING THE WAVES

A conceptual model that reflects the need to work on the present and the future of your organization at the same time is represented by the S-shaped Sigmoid Curve depicted below.

This model describes the natural development of things. For example, some call it a learning curve: people start to learn through trial and error, develop confidence, and achieve mastery. But unless they continue to renew themselves, they become bored and complacent, and performance begins to drop off. The curve can apply to many things, but for our purpose it symbolizes the principle of diminishing returns in the evolution of markets. Quality or marketability or customer interest begins to "max out" after an initial duration of growth.

According to Charles Handy, author of **Beyond Certainty:**

The Sigmoid Curve sums up the story of life itself. We start slowly, experimentally and falteringly, we wax and then we wane. It is the story of the British Empire—and the Russian Empire and of all empires always. It is the story of a product's life-cycle and of many a corporation's rise and fall. It even describes the course of love and of relationships.

In terms of organizational effectiveness, looking at everything in light of the curve could prove depressing: leaders would study where they are on the curve and predict when decline will begin to take place. Organizational life would consist of little more than waiting for the slide to begin, and then trying to turn it around.

The curve experience may be compared to riding a roller coaster. At the beginning as the car goes up, the climb is steep and slow and everyone enjoys the ride. As it approaches the top the whole world opens up, and people smile and enjoy what seems to be a mountain top experience. Then suddenly it plunges over the crest and hurtles downward—and the screaming begins!

Many companies are experiencing the downside of that roller-coaster ride today. Having achieved mastery in their industry, they jubilantly enjoyed success—only to suddenly find themselves frantically fighting with the controls as a sudden decline in market share or customer loyalty drops them off a cliff. Their moment of peak success, which felt so wonderful, proved to be merely the prelude to their plunge into obscurity. Boardroom conversations such as the following abound:

> "Look at these figures. Last year we were celebrating and riding high. Everything was going our way. Yet this is the third straight quarter this year we haven't made our numbers."
>
> "What's going on?"
>
> "I'll tell you what's going on. We need to work harder!"

We suggest a different answer: "I'll tell you what's going on. We need to work smarter." Once you have understood the Sigmoid nature of development, you will realize that you need not wait until a crisis occurs to begin to renew yourself or your organization. Handy adds, "Luckily there is life beyond the curve. The secret of constant growth is to start a new Sigmoid Curve before the first one peters out." The figure on the next page shows you how this might look.

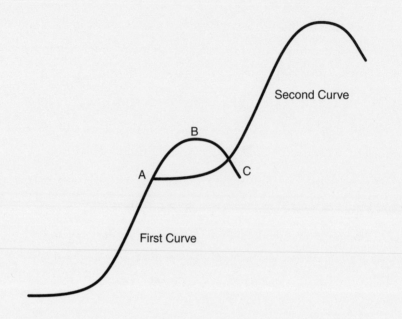

A study of the typical development curve shows that there is wisdom in anticipating the drop-off before it begins to occur. The point on the First Curve designated as A is the "observation point." It is the stage at which a different plan needs to be put into effect. It represents the best time to step back, contemplate one's progress on the curve, and consider launching a new one. By Point B, the slide has already begun. At Point C, it's too late.

COMPARING THE CURVES

W hereas in the past organizations concentrated only upon what they were doing at the time, today's condition of constant change requires that they pay attention not only to improving their present processes (i.e., maintaining the upward thrust of the First Curve) but also designing for the unseen future ahead (i.e., beginning a Second Curve).

In other words, organizations today must have two strategies operating at once. Consider your national postal service. Before the days of e-mail, FEDEX or DHL, and the fax machine, your government probably had a virtual monopoly on the business of transferring information. As these new forms of competition sprang into being, most postal services suddenly found themselves fighting for survival. Delivery cycle times had to be reduced, prices frozen, staff reduced, and service improved. All these initiatives were aimed at trying to keep the postal service in the business of delivering mail; they are examples of First Curve improvements.

First Curve improvement is all about getting better at what you already do. The improvement agenda of the P Team process often revolves around the implementation of a new organizational model, one that comprises fewer layers, faster and more streamlined processes, use of teams, employees more dedicated to constantly questioning everything, and stronger ties with external stakeholders (customers, suppliers, joint ventures, partners). In short, a fast and flexible organization.

The strategies whose purpose is to continuously improve what you already have may help to keep your company afloat today, but they do little to prepare you for the market of tomorrow. And yet, present reality strongly suggests that for the first time in the history of business, a company can be outclassing the competition today and out of business tomorrow.

Let's revisit the case of the postal service. Now it's the 21st century and the Internet is taking off. Suppose that after much study of this new-age communication system, it has become clear that the need for a mail delivery service, regardless of how efficiently it is managed and run, is ending. Mail delivery may become only a fond memory. If so, the postal service will need to engage in Second Curve thinking, fundamental rethinking of what they are in business to do.

It is the mission of the F Team process to build up a Second Curve. While P Teams work on the First Curve by improving the organization's present operation, the Second Curve efforts of F Teams are geared toward trying on various market strategies or organizational models until a good new fit has been found. When that occurs the transition or jump from the First Curve to the Second Curve begins. This ongoing simultaneous approach to both improvement and innovation allows an organization to adapt to environmental change before a crisis has developed. The figure on the next page depicts this process.

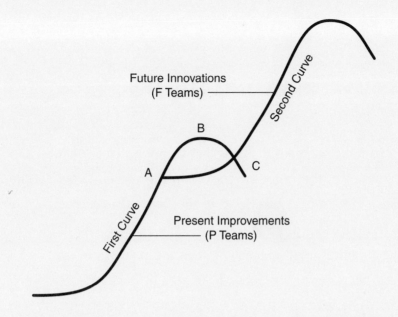

With both teams working in synch, the organization will be utilizing the brain power of all its people. This brings us to our definition of a **world-class organization.**

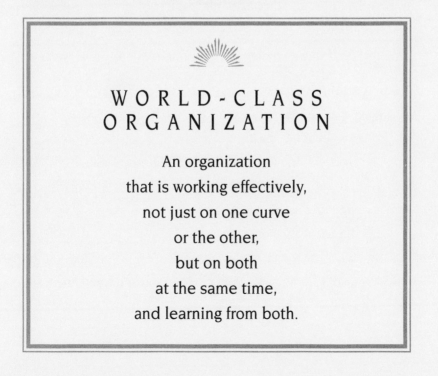

WORLD-CLASS ORGANIZATION

An organization
that is working effectively,
not just on one curve
or the other,
but on both
at the same time,
and learning from both.

REWIRING THE HOUSE

Working on and learning from the two curves simultaneously means that you must allow the past and the future to coexist in the present. Few people have the luxury of being able to shut down their business while they transform it, so they're forced to put up with the turbulence and turmoil characteristic of life between the curves. It will take time for the Second Curve to become established and the First Curve to wane. As a consequence, both curves need to coexist in the same time and space. This could be seen as analogous to rewiring an old house while leaving the electricity on. There is some danger, but if you want electricity throughout the changeover period, you have little choice.

Living between these curves or waves presents leaders with an interesting set of challenges. Chief among these are the need to:

1. Keep the First Curve alive long enough for the Second Curve to firmly establish itself.
2. Develop the perspective and discipline necessary to allow funds to be siphoned away from the curve they currently are leading (the First Curve) to one which they may not be leading (the Second Curve).
3. Be able to live with and manage the confusion and tension that results from having both curves operating simultaneously.

EVOLUTIONARY VS. REVOLUTIONARY CHANGE

W e realize that effectively working on both curves at the same time and learning from each is a difficult assignment. Striving for world-class status is not for the faint of heart. It requires revolutionary change, not evolutionary.

Webster's dictionary defines evolution as "a process of growth or development." Revolution, on the other hand, is defined as "a sudden, radical or complete change...a basic reorientation." Peter Block, in his book **Stewardship,** describes the difference more eloquently:

> Revolution means a turning. Changing direction. *The act of revolving.* It means the change required is significant, obvious even to the casual observer. It is more comforting to talk about evolutionary change. Evolutionary change means that everything is planned, under control, and reasonably predictable.

As we've been suggesting, if you want to have a world-class organization, you must recognize that the difference between these two terms is not merely rhetorical. A butterfly is not just an improved caterpillar but an entirely new creature. Likewise, a revolution is not simply a series of evolutionary steps strung together; it is a break from the past, a discontinuity. And an evolution is not a more gradual form of revolution; it is a gradual process of continuous improvement.

Viewed from the perspective of this book, evolutionary change is one-dimensional. It is limited to movement along the First Curve. It involves building on and improving the present sandcastle. Revolutionary change, on the other hand, is two-dimensional. It requires movement along the First Curve, coupled with the creation of and migration to a Second Curve. It involves keeping the present sandcastle viable as long as possible, while preparing the transition to a completely different dwelling. Thus operational improvements, regardless of their magnitude, are evolutionary. Tinkering with the organizational structure is evolutionary. The reengineering of core processes, and/or the outsourcing of noncore, is evolutionary. However, creatively phasing out the old organizational structure while simultaneously creating a new one is revolutionary

REACTIVE VS. PROACTIVE CHANGE

In Webster's definition of revolution, we saw that the word "sudden" is used. That suggests that revolutionary change is never planned and tends to be reactive rather than proactive. Yet we don't think that is always the case.

There are two ways for leaders to go about changing their organizations. One is to wait until the company hits the wall, in which case they have no choice. That's reactive change. The other way is scan the horizon for opportunity and plot a course to take advantage of it. This is proactive change. The 1984 breakup of AT&T into separate regional companies is an example of the first kind of change; in its case, the wall was the legal system. AT&T had no choice. In 1995, however, the same organization had the information it needed to make the second kind of choice. The company's decision to split itself into three separate companies was voluntary, based squarely on the organization's own best strategic interest. CEO Robert Allen announced "AT&T is reinventing itself once again." The new goal was to get the company ready for tough fights in existing and new markets.

The phrase *"**getting ready**"* is key here. Companies that are getting ready are reassessing what business they are in, who their competitors are, and what their customers want. They are beginning the process of change before they have to. Motorola did that when it decided to get into semiconductors, again when it made the commitment to cellular telephony, and yet again when it conceived itself as a consumer electronics company. J. P. Morgan transformed itself from a commercial bank to an investment bank. The Gap went from a pile-'em-high, sell-'em-cheap retailer of jeans to a retailer of trendy, value-priced fashion basics. And as a final example, there's the Woolworth Corporation which transformed itself from an antiquated dime store and bland discounter into a versatile global specialty retailer.

We're emphasizing this proactive stance in this book because for years it was widely believed that only pain made people change. While we must admit that crisis does provide a strong motivation for change—just think of what happened at Sears and IBM when Wal-Mart and Apple grew into major competitors—we do not believe that crisis thinking is the best way to plot a successful future. It is our hope that you will be able to see the ensuing doom at Observation point A on your First Curve, then begin to manage in a two-curve world.

If you wait until point B or, even worse, point C, to identify your gap, you're already up to your eyeballs in alligators. Now you truly *are* in a reactive change mode. Decisions must be made, and made quickly. And because the company's back is to the wall and everyone knows it, there is even a chance of turning the situation around if everyone pulls together to fight side by side for the company's immediate survival. At best this creates a stressful change effort, one that does not have a high probability of success. W. Stewart Howe, in his book **Corporate Strategy,** contends that for every successful turn-around there are two ailing companies that fail to recover.

We hope corporate leaders are reading this book just in time to proactively scan their business environment in search of unfolding opportunities, while keeping their present operation viable.

THE NEED FOR
A PARTICIPATIVE JOURNEY

Managing in a two-curve world, where you are attempting to improve the present while designing the future, is difficult at best. That fact, combined with the reality that change is a continuous journey, a way of life rather than a one-time event that can be lived through, strengthens our belief that change is something you must do *with* people, not *to* people. This principle becomes particularly important when you believe, as we do, that the change process itself needs to mirror the kind of organization you want to create. Ends must be congruent with means. Thus, if you want to become an organization in which everyone is a partner, everyone must be given an equal opportunity to participate in achieving that. The change process must model partnerships.

Remember that the central purpose behind our plan for involving everyone in the organization in the transformation process—either on a P Team working on First Curve improvements or an F Team focused on Second Curve developments—is the release of energy. When everyone is asked to play an active role in shaping either one curve or the other, extraordinary things can happen.

As Stratford Sherman contends in a **Fortune** magazine article, "A Master Class in Radical Change":

A few pioneers have cut paths through the wilds of revolutionary change. Their experience demonstrates that the process of reinventing an organization is not only possible but also understandable, even predictable.

The diagram below represents our map for the journey.

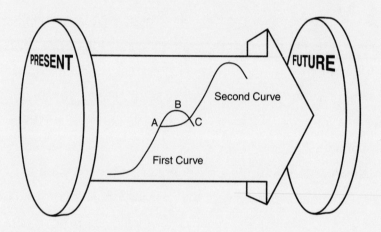

Now that we've laid out the plan and taken a look at it, we can start to get the process under way. Let's begin by considering the whys and some of the hows of making First-Curve improvements.

CHAPTER TWO

REDESIGNING THE CASTLE: FIRST-CURVE IMPROVEMENTS

Nothing stops an organization faster than people who believe that the way they worked yesterday is the best way to work tomorrow. To succeed, not only do your people have to change the way they act, they've got to change the way they think about the past.

Jon Madonna, *Chairman, KPMG International*

Suppose you choose to play on a P team. That means you're more interested in concentrating on improving the present than in designing the future. What is the "present"? We encourage you to give that term your own definition, but for our purposes here we will define the present as **the period between now and eighteen months from now**. For the P Team, the road to the future begins by improving that which already exists—making the company as good as it can possibly be at servicing its present customers in its currently served markets.

In order to get started, you may find it useful to have the organization-wide P Design Team with the help of P Team members think about the following sets of questions.

P Team Questions

The Customer

- Who are our present customers, and why do they buy from us rather than from our competitors?
- Are their needs changing, and if so what is driving those changes?
- How can we use those changes to our advantage?

The Competition

- Who are our present competitors, and why do customers choose them over us?
- Are the rules of engagement changing, and if so what is driving those changes?
- How can we use those changes to our advantage?

Our Company

- If our present customers were to redesign our company for us today, what would they turn us into?

- How can we use the latest technological advances to our advantage?
- How can we strengthen our relationships with our key customers, suppliers, and business partners?

In studying these questions and trying to make sense of the answers that team members throw out in response to them, the team typically will find itself going through a predictable yet challenging sequence of three steps. We call these *Envision, Prepare, Deliver.*

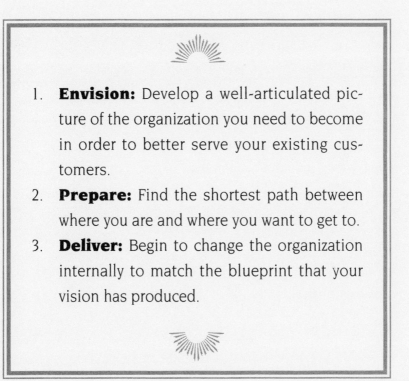

1. **Envision:** Develop a well-articulated picture of the organization you need to become in order to better serve your existing customers.
2. **Prepare:** Find the shortest path between where you are and where you want to get to.
3. **Deliver:** Begin to change the organization internally to match the blueprint that your vision has produced.

Let's look at each of these steps in greater detail.

ENVISION

We have already stated that an organization that still resembles the old sandcastle, with its moat, walls, and tiers, must begin to move in the direction of becoming flat, porous, and inverted. The collective thinking of P Teams must generate a shared vision of the kind of organization you now want to become. What exactly is that vision? **You will know.** We say that simply to remind you that it is your own vision you must come up with. Yet there are strategies to help you to get there. For instance, a visioning process should begin by defining your purpose—what business you are in.

Filling a Need

Your business should be defined, not in terms of the product or service you offer, but in terms of what customer need your product or service fulfills. While products come and go, basic needs and customer groups stay around, i.e., the need for communication, the need for transportation, etc. To allow for the constantly shifting nature of markets, your description of the market need you fulfill should be broad, rather than narrow. To use a classic example, suppose that around the time the automobile was coming into use you'd asked a manufacturer of horse carriages, "What market need do you supply?" If the answer was, "The need for good horse carriages," it's likely that manufacturer would soon have been out of business. Had the same leader answered, "We provide transportation for people," his or her company might have evolved from making horse carriages to making cars, and prospered. Since it's likely that your organization was founded when the landscape was much different than it is today and times were stable, you must decide whether what you think you do still makes sense. If not, you have to decide what you ought to be doing.

In developing a market-based (rather than product-based) business definition, you should avoid arriving at too narrow a statement. For instance, if you're an investment company and you think you're in the stocks and bonds business, you could be out of business soon. With the coming of the information highway, everybody on your block has instant access to the same information any broker has. But as soon as you visualize your business as financial planning, suddenly you could be looking at a long-term future. By widening the scope of your services to your customers, you're throwing out a bigger fishnet.

Here are some more examples of product-based versus customer-based definitions:

- FROM a garage opener company TO providing easy access in and out of buildings
- FROM a training and development company TO a consulting services company
- FROM a telephone company TO a communications provider

Some actual companies who have made the switch:

	FROM	TO
SAS	We run an airline.	We transport people and goods.
Xerox	We make office equipment.	We help improve office productivity.
Hoover	We make vacuums.	We help create cleaner and healthier environments.
Midas	We make mufflers.	We provide complete auto servicing.

Note that when you move from thinking about a specific product to the **purpose** of that product your horizon expands. Regardless of the product, people will always have concerns about transportation, office productivity, keeping their homes clean and healthy, and servicing their cars. What you don't want to get caught doing is producing a product or service that people no longer want. For many of you this may seem elementary; for others it could be big news!

When you think, *What business are we in?* ask yourself:

- What are our principal products or services?
- What are some possible substitutes for these?
- Why do customers buy these products or services?
- What are the principal benefits they expect from these purchases?

Corporate Profiling

Once you've clarified the customer need or needs your business supplies, now think about how you've shaped (or *will* shape) your organization to meet these needs. To do this corporate profiling you need to study the interaction of a number of key factors. It's through the interaction of these business elements that you will provide your product or service to the customer.

Mary Gelinas and Roger James as part of their **Collaborative Organizational Design** developed a visual model that identifies the critical elements of an organization that are constantly interacting with a changing business environment. We will use this model to help you understand what is involved in corporate profiling.

Elements of Organization

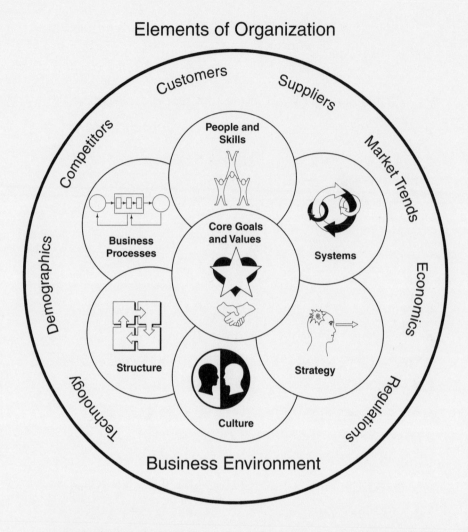

Now let's define each of the elements you see in the Gelinas and James model.

CORE GOALS are broad notions of future direction, the fundamental accomplishments the organization wants to achieve. As an organization, what thing or things are you in the world to do? Your answers will lead you to your core goals. Core goals define the reason you exist—your mission or purpose. They are broad statements of intent, often framed in terms of time, the accomplishment of which will provide constant reinforcement of your mission. Your core goals symbolize and express your core values. For example, the medical center at Vanderbilt University has this as one of its core goals: *Creation of an integrated and comprehensive regional health care delivery system.* Levi-Strauss & Co. has a core goal of *sustaining responsible commercial success*. "Responsible" means conducting its business ethically and demonstrating leadership in satisfying its responsibilities to its community and to society.

CORE VALUES are what the organization stands for, holds dear. Values are the heart and soul of an organization. They are the fundamental notions of ideal behavior, the set of beliefs upon which decisions are made and actions taken. Strictly speaking, values are the "what's really important" in an organization, and newcomers soon learn the values simply by observing behavior.

Values statements can provide important guidelines for redirecting behavior, especially during periods of organizational change. Stated values can be rich with significance, depending on management's commitment to "walking their talk." For a while organizations may listen, and even agree, to what managers say, but in the long run they believe what managers *do*. If employees feel that managers are saying one thing and doing another, cynicism sets in, and value statements become meaningless. For this reason we are advocates of **Managing By Values® (MBV)**.

What does it mean to manage by values? In Blanchard and O'Connor's book **Managing By Values: Becoming a Fortunate 500 Company**, the authors identify three MBV steps.

1. **Identifying Core Values.** Managing By Values begins by identifying a core set of operating values. Lots of companies claim they have a set of core values, but what they mean is a list of generic business beliefs that everyone would agree with such as having integrity, making a profit, responding to customers, etc. Such God-mother-and-country values have meaning only when they are (a) further defined in terms of how people actually will behave and (b) are rank-ordered to reveal priority.

   For example, Disney's four core values for their theme parks are, in order of importance, **safety, courtesy, the show** (performing according to the requirements of your particular role), and **efficiency.** If these values hadn't been so carefully ordered, people would in effect have been left to their own devices. For example, a bottom-line–oriented manager might overemphasize efficiency and thus jeopardize the three higher-ranking values.

2. **Communicating Core Values.** This step involves making sure

that your values are evident to all stakeholders—employees, customers, suppliers, stockholders, and the community. The core values of Norstan, a telecommunications company head-quartered in Minneapolis, are found in the adjectives **ethical, responsive, profitable,** in that order. Any opportunity that arises for Norstan to trumpet forth its values, it seizes upon. These values appear on framed posters throughout the company's corporate headquarters and regional facilities. Every business card highlights them, as well as corporate brochures and reports.

3. **Aligning Values and Practices.** Without some method of identifying gaps between values and behavior, a set of core values is nothing more than a wish list. Eighty percent of the time allotted for implementing the Managing By Values process is given over to the alignment stage. Clarifying the values gives you a new way to view problems: as violations of your values. Once you start looking, all you seem to find are the gaps. When Blanchard Training and Development, Inc., instituted the MBV process, employees elected ombudspeople, both managers and nonmanagers, to help facilitate a process of identifying and closing the gaps between core values and organizational practices/procedures, as well as people's behavior.

STRATEGY is one's approach to achieving a sense of mission. It's asking: "Now that we know our core goals, how are we going to accomplish them?" Strategy is sometimes defined as the way a company plans to create unique value.

To create unique value, each company must follow its own

strategy. There are as many different strategies as there are companies. According to consultants Michael Treacy and Fred
Wiersema, in their book *The Disciplines of Market Leaders,*
there are three value disciplines on which a company may
focus: (1) organizational efficiency, (2) product innovation, or
(3) customer intimacy. Their observations suggest that world-
class companies generally are great at one of these disciplines
and pretty good at the other two.

1. *Organizational Efficiency.* A company pursuing this strategy
   works hard to achieve the lowest costs of production and distribution, so that it can price lower than its competitors. Two companies that follow this strategy are Wal-Mart and Dell Computer.
   While these organizations don't emphasize product or service
   innovation or cultivating deep-down relationships with customers as their principal discipline, neither do they neglect
   them. For example, Wal-Mart focused on customer intimacy
   when they planted friendly and informed greeters at their store's
   front doors.

2. *Product Innovation.* A company pursuing this strategy focuses
   on providing the best product. It is continually leading the market with new breakthrough products. Nike, given the blazing
   speed with which it introduces new products, has practically
   taken over the market in their field. McDonald's is similar; it
   was the first fast-food chain to introduce breakfast, and it led the
   way with healthier choices. Can these organizations afford to be
   blasé about cost or customer relations? Of course not. They're
   simply not their major areas of emphasis.

3. *Customer Intimacy.* Customer-driven companies strive to make "raving fans" of their customers. In their interactions with their customers they want to create service stories that will have these customers bragging about the service they received. Nordstrom and Disney focus on this strategy. Nordstrom's legendary "no-problem" return policy, and the universal friendliness and attentiveness of Disney's employees, keep people talking about them and coming back for more. It is a Nordstrom company policy that it will match the price on an item that can be bought more cheaply at another store. Yet they don't advertise this policy because competing on cost is not their key strategy.

Which of these three strategic approaches does your firm now emphasize? You need to choose a primary strategy without neglecting the other two. For example, an investment company might divide its business into two separate entities, one a product division and the other a financial planning division. The emphasis in the product division would be on product innovation, followed by organizational efficiency, with customer intimacy being the last concern. In the financial planning division, customer intimacy would lead the way, followed by product innovation, with organizational efficiency receiving the least emphasis. In both cases the two lesser concerns cannot be ignored. For example, you can have the greatest product in the world but if your systems are antiquated and people can't get what they want when they want it, after a while your product quality won't be able to carry the day on its own.

Why is it important to develop a primary strategy? Because it provides a differentiated platform on which to compete, and beams the energies of your work force in a single direction. The firm that fails to develop its strategy in at least one of the three directions we have indicated is probably limping along with an unmotivated work force.

BUSINESS PROCESSES. Your organization has many inter-connected activities that enable you to reach your goals; these are your business processes. Inputs (materials, capital, and people) are used, deliverables (products and services) are produced, and customer satisfaction and/or feedback are used to continuously improve things. The business processes at Levi-Strauss & Co. involve all the pieces of the supply chain. To them that means finding a product idea, designing the product, creating it, and delivering it. At Vanderbilt University's Medical Center, the key process phrases are access/intake, diagnosis, treatment, and exit/follow-up.

STRUCTURE is defined by the characteristic forms through which people relate to each other and to the work flow. Structure includes the following components, among others:

- Definition of departments, units, etc.
- Levels of supervision/management
- Job/work design
- Span of supervisory control
- Delegation of authority
- Physical layout

The elements of formal structure include individual jobs, subunits (teams, departments, divisions), and a management hierarchy. These design tools generally are used to influence behavior by clearly specifying what various individuals should be responsible for, where in the organization and with and for whom they should work, and what authority they should have.

Structure is a key determinant of whether a company can be fast and flexible. One of the reasons Wal-Mart was able to waltz right by the traditional giant Sears was that there were only 3 management layers between Sam Walton's leadership and a cashier, as against Sears, 12 levels of hierarchy. If a new product idea came to Wal-Mart, they could have it on the shelves within 30 days—the time it took Sears to finish appointing a committee to study it. Sears has made some significant improvements in recent years because of the reality of this competitive edge and is coming back as a strong competitor.

Like strategies, organizational structures come in many varieties, yet most can be grouped under one of the following categories:

The Functional Structure. This is your typical pyramidal hierarchy. From atop the wedding-cake-shaped hierarchy, the leader looks down on order, symmetry, and uniformity, a neat step-by-step distribution of the company's tasks and responsibilities. From the bottom, frontline managers look up at a series of filters and controllers whose demands soak up most of their energies and time. This structure may make sense when you're starting a new enterprise, when a founder has a vision, dream, or plan in his/her head and needs lieutenants to carry it out.

The Product–Market–Geographic Area Structure. This structure is a close cousin of the functional hierarchy. The key difference here is the grouping of jobs. Under the functional structure, all marketing or finance or personnel jobs or subunits are grouped into their own specific departments. In the case of the product–market–geographic area structure, however, all jobs or subunits dealing with the same product or service are grouped into departments or geographical areas. For example, all jobs or subunits dealing with Europe are grouped into the European division, etc., regardless of their function such as finance, marketing, etc.

The Matrix Structure. A product of the 1960s, the matrix structure has experienced a resurgence of interest lately. In this model an individual or work group is structurally subject to the direction of two bosses, one typically representing a functional concern and the other a product or service concern. For example, ABB's global matrix requires the managers of each frontline unit to report to both a regional manager and a worldwide business head. Why is this structure attracting renewed interest? According to ABB's CEO and president, Percy Barnevik, it allows his organization "to be simultaneously global and local, big and small, centralized and decentralized."

The Flat Structure. The surge of downsizing in recent years is an attempt to flatten traditional structures and limit the layers of hierarchy, so as to be fast and flexible in response to market changes and customer demands. *Warning:* Don't assume that flattening is a panacea, unless it goes along with a basic change in management philosophy. A number of large corporations that have downsized have simply become smaller bureaucracies.

The Inverted Pyramid. Most great organizations start with a visionary leader at the top who has a dream for the business and energizes others to pursue it. Once the vision and direction are set, problems begin when managers throughout the organization want to keep the hierarchy alive and well. This means they perceive themselves as responsible, and everybody below them should be responsive to their whims and wishes. Decision making is slowed and the organization's effectiveness is diminished.

These days, it's when frontline people can solve problems on the spot that organizations are seen as fast and flexible. One way to overcome the limitations of the functional structure is to philosophically turn the pyramid upside down, so that frontline or customer-contact people are on the top and top managers are on the bottom. When it comes to implementation and accomplishment, this way of thinking can make a traditional functional hierarchy more effective because of its responsiveness to the customer. Now managers are responsive to their people (getting information to them, seeing that they have the resources they need, supporting them), and their people are responsible (able to respond).

Self-Directed Teams. This structure takes the form of numerous flexible, relatively permanent work teams whose most important relationships are horizontal: with suppliers, customers, and peers. Each team consists of a group of employees with the responsibility for an entire process, product, or customer relationship. They plan, perform, and manage the work from start to finish. While a group may have a manager or "coach," everyone shares equally in the responsibilities.

For example, a customer team would be the sensing arm of the organization when it comes to that customer and the problem-solving resource for that customer. Its members would be concerned with anything that goes wrong in the company's efforts to serve that customer. When an error occurs, they would immediately gather all information about it and feed it to the production and billing operations so these people understand what has been done wrong and can correct it. If it is a cross-functional team, it would even have members from production and billing.

This group functions in ways only managers did in the past: assessing information, then acting in a responsible way that keeps everyone informed. Blanchard, Carlos, and Randolph, in their book **Empowerment Takes More Than A Minute,** see self-directed work teams as a conceivable replacement for the hierarchy.

The Networking Organization. Today everyone is talking about strategic alliances. Like building contractors who manage contracts but depend on subcontracts with carpenters, electricians, plumbers, masons, and other specialists, leaders are realizing that the world is too complicated to make it on their own. Thus they are experimenting with various ways to network with individuals and groups that can make their operations more effective. These alliances may be internal (between departments within the same organization) or external (with other organizations, even competitors).

This structure is totally flexible in that it is comprised of few, if any, fixed teams or relationships. Within its porous, and ever changing boundaries, insiders and outsiders alike are constantly engaged in a complex dance ritual in which teams are assembled, disassembled, and then reassembled around specific work projects. People working on these teams typically have no real home base and may actually serve on numerous teams at the same time. These teams may be part of the new virtual organization where some or all team members are temporary and not even employees. This form of structure is especially common within consulting firms, internal staff groups, and within organizations pursuing either mass customization or globalization strategies, where the emphasis is on increasing customer value while reducing time, cost, and risk.

All these various structures have strengths and weaknesses, as well as degrees of relevance to today's economy. Looking at how you are organized has to be an ongoing process. As competition and external conditions change, so must you. Restructuring an organization can no longer be thought of as a one-time deal. Rather, it's an ongoing process, dictated by the changing needs in the business environment. The dramatic reorganization of AT&T in the fall of 1995 that we talked about earlier is a good example of this. The new structure divided AT&T into three focused pieces, each staying out of the way of the other two—one branch to sell long-distance and communications services, another to make communications equipment such as phones and switches, and a third to be a computer company. The interrelationship between strategy and structure in this move is unmistakable.

SYSTEMS are the procedures, formal and informal, that make the organization go. They support the structure.

Bob Lorber, co-author of **Putting the One Minute Manager to Work** and noted consultant, uses five systems in his performance improvement work. Systems like these must be in place if an organization is to function at a high level.

1. *Accountability.* In order for an organization's goals to be reached, every person, whether working individually or in a work group, needs to know what he or she will be held accountable for. All good performance starts with clear goals. The clearer you make each goal—spelling out exactly what will be done, by whom, by when, how successful achievement will be measured, and what good performance looks

like—the more accountable you are making the person or persons who will carry it out.

2. ***Data/Information Systems.*** Given today's explosion of information, the effective managing and disseminating of information can itself become a key strategy. When we talk about data systems, we're talking about ways to get people information on finances, customer feedback, performance—anything that supports them in effective decision making. People without pertinent information cannot self-monitor or make sound decisions; people with information can.

3. ***Feedback.*** For a long while now customer service trainer Rick Tate has been saying that "feedback is the breakfast of champions." Can you imagine trying out for the Olympics as a sprinter and then nobody will give you your times? Without feedback, people have no way of knowing whether performance is on the mark or falling short. Given the wide array of information technologies available today, there is simply no excuse for denying people information relevant to their performance. Relevant feedback is important for problem identification, coaching, and performance evaluation.

4. ***Recognition.*** In *The One Minute Manager,* Blanchard and Johnson say, "Catch people doing something right." Most organizations accent the negative, but when people know their good side is showing they rise to the occasion and even begin to shore up their weaknesses. The rapid acceptance of Bob Nelson's book ***1001 Ways to Reward Employees*** showed how vital it is to recognize people's

performance. A good recognition system is invaluable for compensation and promotion decisions.

5. ***Training.*** Training is a key strategy when it comes to making any company a learning organization. The second most common reason, after unclear goals, why people fail in their jobs is lack of training. Every change in an organization's structure or systems will require training. To assume that people will know what to do, or will find out on their own, is simply to ask for trouble. Also, the flattening of organizations requires cross-training so that the organization can flexibly respond to its demands. If you walk into a place of business and find that almost anyone there can solve your problem, it's certain that company has been using the cross-training strategy.

PEOPLE AND SKILLS refers to the types of professions and skills that must be possessed by the people in the organization if its established goals are to be reached. It also has to do with the need, potential, and resources/methodologies for skill and capability development.

Before you can identify the kinds of people you need in your organization, you must determine the core skills your organization requires if it is to implement your agreed-upon strategy and reach its stipulated goals.

Core Skills. Gary Hamel and C. K. Prahalad, authors of ***Competing for the Future,*** use the phrase operational competencies to describe core skills. They define these as being "a cluster of skills and technologies which collectively make a disproportionate and competitively unique contribution to customer-perceived value, and in so doing serve as a source of competitive advantage."

As stated, the core skills a company needs are unique to that organization. Consequently there is much variability between companies. Consider the following examples:

Honda   Honda's core skill in engines and power trains gives it a distinctive advantage in car, motorcycle, lawn mower, and generator business.

Canon   Canon's core skill in optics, imaging, and microprocessor controls have enabled it to enter and even dominate markets as seemingly diverse as copiers, laser printers, cameras, and image scanners.

3M   3M's core skill in sticky tape has equipped it to compete in businesses as diverse as pressure-sensitive tape, magnetic tape, photographic film, and post-it notes.

Casio   Casio consolidated corporate-wide technologies and production skills into core skills in miniaturization, microprocessor design, and ultrathin precision casing. These skills have enabled the company to produce competitive miniature radios, pocket TVs, digital watches, and miniature card   calculators.

Because core skills are unique to each company, you and your leaders must compile your own list of operational competencies. The process can be quite time consuming. In fact, according to Hamel and Prahalad, "The time it takes to arrive at an insightful, creative, and shared definition of core competencies is, in a large company, more likely to be measured in months than weeks." Upon its completion, however, the final list should contain anywhere from five to ten items, each of which should meet the following criteria.

- An integration of a variety of individual skills and technologies
- Something competitors cannot easily imitate
- An attribute unique to the organization
- Ability to make a sizable contribution to customer-perceived value
- An item essential to corporate survival in both the short term and the long term
- Ability to serve as a gateway into new markets

People. Core skills need people to put them into action. There are four key human resource functions involved in getting the right people into the right jobs at the right time.

1. **Recruiting and Hiring.** It used to be that organizations valued skills, long experience, loyalty, and obedience. Nowadays there is no job security. It is estimated that in the future people will have five or more "careers" in the course of their lifetimes. When a person changes companies, the skills and experience gained in the former position may not fit the new core competencies.

48

2. ***Training and Development.*** Job security is a thing of the past. No longer do people want to be treated like mushrooms: kept in the dark, given occasional nourishment with fertilizer, and expected to grow. What people want from a company is the training that will teach them new skills that will help them to add value wherever they are.

3. ***Coaching and Evaluation.*** Possessing clear goals and having relevant training are important ingredients of success, but they only kick off the process. What really develops people is day-to-day coaching: having high expectations and following up with constant monitoring and feedback, with praise for progress and immediate corrections to stay on course as needed. Without day-to-day coaching, evaluation is based on a few shots in the dark.

4. ***Career Planning.*** In the past, career planning was viewed as a strategy for climbing the organizational ladder. Now with the elimination of layers and the downplaying of political/hierarchical structures, career planning is based on a new contract: As the employee adds value, the company provides opportunities for him/her to develop new skills and experience that will be marketable anywhere.

The problem in most companies is that these functions are performed by different groups who don't talk to each other. Integrating these functions should become a goal if you want to increase the skills and capabilities of your people.

CULTURE refers to the norms of an organization, "the way we do things around here." It is reflected in people's behavior and language. An organization's culture is deep and complex, and based on the shared assumptions and beliefs of its members. These assumptions and beliefs often are unconscious and taken for granted. Culture is a product of group experience, found where there is a definable group with some history. Style of leadership is the primary driver in creating culture. It is a function of how decisions are made, communication flows, information is shared, motivation is generated, and conflict is handled.

If a stranger were to ask the people in your organization, "How are things done around here?" he or she soon would be swamped with stories and opinions. These would be pieces of the culture. The culture would be the sum total of the informational artifacts gathered from conversations among stakeholders. If leaders would listen carefully to the talk going on in halls, parking lots, and rest rooms, they would gain valuable insights into the culture of their companies.

It's also important for leaders to ask, "Is our culture a driving or a restraining force for change?" Whether your culture supports or resists change very often is a function of the leadership style practiced throughout the organization. Every manager has his or her unique way of influencing others.

Developing Your Improvement Vision

In developing an improvement vision, members of your organization-wide P Design Team and its corresponding P Teams want to consider each of these elements in the light of the question: ***What would our ideal state be in respect to this element if our organization were maximizing its potential?***

This would involve pondering the following:

- Why does this organization exist? (purpose)
- What are we trying to accomplish? (core goals)
- What do we stand for? (core values)
- What is our basic approach to achieving our purpose? (strategy)
- How should we be organized? (structure)
- What will be our operating procedures? (systems and business processes)
- What kind of staff and competencies (people and skills) will be needed, and how do we want them to behave? (culture)

This is not an easy task. In fact, it could seem overwhelming. All of your P Team people should actively participate with the organization- wide P Design Team in answering these questions. Eventually you will need the help of F Team members and their Design Team, too. To gain people's commitment to any change, all who could be impacted by it must come on board. Whatever vision is developed, it should reflect the aspirations of everyone in your organization as well as the needs (present and pending) of the market. This means the P Team process must have kept everyone informed step-by-step at all levels.

PREPARE

Once your purpose is clear and the overall picture of all the elements of the organization is in place, you're ready to enter the "prepare" step. Here your organization-wide P Design Team is charged with the task of finding the shortest path between where you are now and where you want to get to in the near future. One of the best ways to do that is to scrutinize what successful companies already are doing. P Team members would be well suited for this "best practices" assignment.

Five Emerging Characteristics

As we have traveled around the world and worked with various companies and industries, it has become evident to us that there are five key characteristics of effective companies, organizations that are outstripping the competition and setting the mark for excellence in their industries. In order to depict these key characteristics, we have chosen to use the familiar three-legged stool, the kind that farmers have rested their weary bottoms on down through the centuries when milking cows. We like this stool metaphor for two reasons. First, farmers used this stool for milking because of its stability. Whether the ground was flat, uneven, or sloped the stool never toppled over. This suggests that the conceptual stool model has the stability to serve in all kinds of organizational circumstances and business environments. Second, the strength of a three-legged stool depends on all three legs being solid. If even one of the legs is weak, the stool collapses. By using the stool as our model of key characteristics we are suggesting that each of the three key aspects of organizational effectiveness must be solidly in place, held up by the seat of **integrity** and surrounded by an environment characterized by **continuous improvement.**

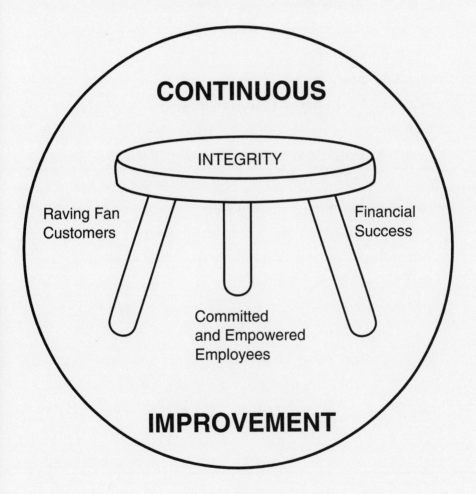

As the figure on the preceding page shows, the three "legs" we see strong organizations relying on are **raving fan customers, committed and empowered employees,** and **financial success.**

Raving Fan Customers

These days nobody has to convince anybody that the customer is king. Competition is everywhere. Organizational leaders are realizing that they are nowhere without the loyalty and commitment of their customers. The world has changed in such a way that today the buyer, not the seller, is sitting in the driver's seat. Companies are motivated to change when they discover the new rule: **If you don't take care of your customers, somebody else will.**

Ken Blanchard and Sheldon Bowles, in their book **Raving Fans: Satisfied Customers Are Not Good Enough,** argue that to keep your customers today you can't be content just to satisfy them; you have to create "raving fans." They describe raving fans as being customers who are so excited about the way you treat them that they want to tell everyone about you; they become part of your sales force. Let's look at an example.

An elderly woman goes to her refrigerator to get some ice. When she opens the ice section, water comes pouring out; something clearly is wrong. Going to the Yellow Pages, she calls appliance service companies one after the other, only to be told that the earliest anyone can visit her is in three weeks. Discouraged, she's about to call her son for help when she sees a little ad that says, "Same Day Service." She calls the number, and soon a friendly voice is saying, "Sure, we'd be happy to fix your refrigerator today. When would you like us to come?" "I have a choice?" the woman responds in amazement. "How about two o'clock?"

Not only does a serviceman show up at two, he even has tools and knows what a refrigerator is. He fixes the fridge and as he's leaving he hands his business card to his happy customer. It has his home phone number on the back. "Anytime, night or day, you have a problem with this refrigerator, you can give me a call." What do you think this woman does for the next three days? She calls everyone she knows to tell them about the service she has received. She has become a ***raving fan***.

Raving fans are created by companies whose service far exceeds that of the competition, and even customers' expectations. These companies routinely do the unexpected, and then enjoy the growth generated by customers who have spontaneously joined their sales force.

Committed and Empowered Employees

You will get little argument today if you tell managers that people are their most important resource. Some even argue that the customer should come second, because without committed and empowered employees, good service can never be provided. You can't treat your people poorly and expect them to treat your customers well.

Why exactly are your people so important today? Because these days your organization is evaluated on how quickly it can respond to customer needs and problems. "I'll have to talk to my boss" doesn't cut it any more. Nobody cares who the boss is. The only people customers care about are the ones who answer the phone, greet them, write up their order, make their delivery, or respond to their complaints. They want top service, and they want it fast. That means you need to have committed and empowered people working for you.

To achieve this, you should take a look at your organizational structure. In their book, **The Flight of the Buffalo**, Ralph Stayer and Jim Belasco make some important points about the impact of structure on flexibility and the capacity of organizations to empower their work forces. The reason hunters in the Old West were able to kill thousands of buffalo was that all they had to do was chase the lead buffalo off a cliff, and the rest of the buffalo would follow. The authors' conclusion is that although such buffalo behavior served as a model for Industrial Age decision making, in this new fast-paced Information Age it has some important limitations.

The analogy that Stayer and Belasco like best is the flock of geese. As you've probably observed, geese travel in a V pattern, with the leader out in front. When that bird gets tired, another assumes the leadership role. If you had a big enough horizon, in time you would see all the birds take the leadership position. Another thing that is attractive about geese is that they are willing to change their structure if the task changes. While a V structure is effective for flying, it would lead to disaster if utilized for landing. Consequently, they form a new structure and peel off one at a time.

The point here is: Don't get trapped within your organizational structure. In fact, if you have an organizational chart, you might consider throwing it away. If it's up on the wall, people will think they're supposed to be in those boxes; the familiar refrain, "That's not my job!" will soon be floating through the halls. Take the chart down. Then if your shipping department is overloaded in a single day and you ask members of your accounting department to go over and help (since it's the beginning of the month and their workload is lighter), they won't question it. Empowered and committed employees, ready and willing to go and help whenever and wherever they are needed, make the critical difference in maintaining old customers and attracting new ones.

Financial Success

No matter how well you treat your customers and employees, if your company is hemorrhaging cash, it won't survive for long. The basic law of economics requires sales to exceed expenses. This puts companies in a difficult balancing act: They have to wow customers, but do so without giving away the store.

Large bureaucratic organizations grew up at a time when

money wasn't much of a problem. Today the prize goes to those who can do more with less. The margins in some businesses are so thin it's hard to imagine how they can be profitable. For example, a high tech product like a small cellular phone that might have initially cost the consumer over a thousand dollars, within a short period of time is wanted for under a hundred dollars and at a higher quality!

More companies are deciding that the only way for them to be financially effective today is to downsize. There's no doubt that some personnel reduction is necessary in large bureaucracies where everyone just had to have an assistant, and then the assistant had to have an assistant. Yet downsizing is by no means the only way to manage costs. There's a growing realization that another important way is to make all of your people your business partner. For instance, in some companies, new people can't get a raise until they can read their company's balance sheet and understand where and how their individual efforts are impacting the company's profit-and-loss statement. When people understand the business realities of how their organization makes money, they are much more apt to roll up their sleeves and help out.

Traditionally, managers have been reluctant to share financial information. But these days "open-book management" is a response being made by companies who have realized what large financial gains can be made by sharing previously "sensitive" data. For example, in working with a restaurant company a consultant was having a hard time convincing the president of the merits of sharing important financial data with employees. To unfreeze the president's thinking, the consultant went to the firm's biggest restaurant one night at closing time. Dividing all the employees—cooks, dishwashers, waiters and waitresses, bus people, receptionist—into groups of five or six, he asked them to come to agreement about the answer to a question: "Of every sales dollar that comes into this restaurant, how many cents do you think fall to the bottom line—money that can be returned to investors as profit or reinvested in the business?"

The least amount any group guessed was forty cents. Several groups guessed seventy cents. (In a restaurant the reality is that if you can keep five cents on the dollar, you get excited—ten cents and you're ecstatic!) Can you imagine the attitude among employees toward such things as food costs, labor costs, and breakage when they thought their company was a money machine? After sharing the actual figures, the president was impressed when a chef asked, "You mean if I burn a six-dollar steak, we have to sell at least twenty more steaks for essentially no profit to make up for my wastage?" He already had things figured out.

Another approach to financial success that some organizational leaders are taking is determining which of their departments are cost centers and which are profit centers. Once leaders have identified their cost centers (accounting and personnel typically are cost centers these days), they are asking a followup question: "Is there a strategic reason why we are performing this function?" If not, the thought is that maybe that function needs to be outsourced to another company—one that makes a profit by doing that work. It is estimated that corporate leaders are spending most of their time solving problems associated with their cost centers and little time trying to increase sales in their profit centers.

The Need for Balance between the Three Legs

In the past several decades, many companies have behaved as though financial success could support the stool on its own. However, as customers and employees alike have grown increasingly migratory, these companies have had to reorder their priorities.

We believe that profit is the result of keeping paramount the needs and concerns of your employees and customers. It's the applause you get from raving fan customers and committed and empowered employees. As management consultant and author Ichak Adizes often says, "Managing only for profit is like playing tennis with your eye on the scoreboard and not on the ball." In this case, the ball represents your relationship with customers and people. We think if you pay attention to these, financial success will follow.

Integrity

Having identified and labeled each of the legs of the stool, we are left with the seat itself. The seat represents organizational integrity: Does the organization walk its talk? Are its decisions and actions value-driven? On the first page of almost every annual report we see, the importance of customers and employees is stressed; yet when we examine more closely the company's policies, procedures, and practices, we quickly discover large gaps between what the organization says and what it does.

For example, any company that espouses the importance of customers should have an all-out recovery strategy in place for when things go wrong, yet in most cases when customers complain about service they're put under a hot lamp and interrogated as if they were criminals. The same gaps occur with employees. Many companies may say their people are important, but they still employ a normal-distribution policy. You know how that works. When it comes to evaluating performance—only a few people can score high, a few people must be rated low, and the bulk of the evaluations fall in the middle. By contrast, the actions of value-driven companies clearly reflect their stated beliefs; if they say their customers and people are important, they also act as if they are.

Continuous Improvement

The circle surrounding the stool in the diagram is there to delineate the need for an ongoing process that keeps all parts of the stool strong and stable and permits it to function well. This is the process of continuous improvement. If an organization isn't improving, it's getting worse; there is simply no standing still.

This means that learning must become the organization's way of life. Just as in the case of individuals, the only way to have job security is to learn new skills. So too the only way organizations can be assured of having a future is to be better tomorrow than today, better next week than this week, better next year than this year.

If continuous improvement is truly to take place, learning from mistakes must be more important than determining whose fault something was. 3M became legendary for shooting off a cannon whenever anyone made a mistake. Why did they do it? They were celebrating a learning opportunity. In **Everyone's A Coach,** Don Shula, the winningest coach in National Football League history, says that as a coach he wanted his players to come out of every meeting, practice, and game knowing more than they did when they went in. Shula's attitude toward losses was summed up in his motto: "Success is not forever, and failure isn't fatal." He gave himself and his team only 24 hours to celebrate a victory or mourn a defeat. During that 24 hours he wanted everyone to learn all they could about what had worked or had failed to work. After that he wanted all of his team's attention focused on the next game, and not on looking back.

Gap Analysis

Once a "Best Practices" study has been completed by P Team members, now your organization-wide P Design Team should lead a comprehensive gap analysis, identifying discrepancies between the vision and the organization's present state. Its first task is to gather data about the present state of things. This will be collected by P Teams all over the organization. Once data gathering has been completed, the P Design Team will serve as a resource for the Steering Committee, as they come to agreement on the major changes that need to be made.

It's important at this point to realize that you can't change everything at once. All the research on peak performance indicates that people do best when they focus on doing a few things well. We're all familiar with the 80-20 rule: Eighty percent of the performance you want to achieve will come out of twenty percent of what you do. Effective change depends upon focused energy—doing the right things well. How do you determine what are the right things to do? Your focus should be arrived at by comparing your vision of perfection for each of the organizational elements with the data your teams have gathered in the diagnostic stage. Which of these elements needs your attention first? The "best practices" study should be helpful here.

If you were to try to change all the elements at once, you'd be ineffective. For example, in redesigning its operation, a training and development company arrived at the proper focus for their P Teams' efforts through a perusal of all its elements. They generally were pleased with their core goals and values, people skills and strategies, but they too frequently found themselves in a recovery stage with customers and suppliers because their structure, internal processes, and systems proved inadequate to match their rapid growth and changing customer needs and demands. Therefore, they decided that their initial change efforts should focus on structure, business processes and systems. Doing things right the first time had to be the goal. If some basic changes were made in these elements, they felt the culture would automatically shift in the desired direction.

If you compare your present operation with how you want to perform in the key organizational areas, you will quickly identify where the gaps are the widest. Improvement must begin there and other changes will follow from this work. Organizational redesign is like fixing a car. On the surface it may seem that your problem is simply the exhaust system, but when it is replaced and more back pressure is placed on the engine, other parts may show signs of wear and lack of efficiency. Similarly, once your P Design Team and Steering Committee have begun to address obvious deficiencies in a couple of organizational areas, you will notice gaps in other places that you hadn't before realized were critical.

Since all the elements are in dynamic interaction with each other, this is as it should be. Identifying the gaps establishes the need for change. Now sponsors and champions must come forward to take the lead in change efforts. Rather than depending on top management, recruitment of change leaders must go on at all levels. (An obvious place to look is within the P Teams.) Identifying emerging leaders throughout the organization will help to build its commitment and capacity to change, as well as ensure the design of a customer-focused, comprehensive, collaborative change process.

DELIVER

The deliver step is all about implementation. When all the significant gaps have been identified and decisions made about what has to be done, the change process begins. In fact a change effort is only necessary when there is a difference between what is presently happening and what you would like to be happening. As a result, change is always a product of dissatisfaction.

No Step-by-Step Formula

Since managing in constantly churning white water is a reality, many of you doubtless are anxious to know exactly where to begin and how to proceed with your change efforts. The truth of the matter is that neither we, nor anyone else for that matter, can provide you with a generic road map for managing change. Each transformational journey must follow its own unique path. Corporate change paths are like fingerprints and snowflakes—no two are ever the same. The best that we can do is describe some of the landmarks and important issues you are likely to encounter along the way. Some of these include:

- **Holistic View.** Involving many people, all with differing views and perspectives, ensures that a more complete picture of the organization's realities and opportunities can be constructed. This eclectic mix of individual perspectives is critical; no one person, nor group of people for that matter, can ever know it all.

- **Pace of Change.** Having everyone simultaneously and actively engaged in the change process dramatically quickens the organization's capacity to change. Because so many get behind the change process at the same time, momentum builds quickly. Everyone hears the same message at the same time. Distortions and delays are reduced to a minimum.

- **Ownership of the Change Process.** Ownership resides with those who create, and with them alone. The degree of ownership people have in any change effort is directly proportional to their level of involvement. The more involved they are in deciding upon which changes need to be made, and how they are to be made, the more apt they are to understand the need for the changes and to commit to making them. We stress that the relevant model today is "Everyone's a change agent."

- **Participative vs. Directive Change.** When we say this to people, they usually think we are proponents of participative change and against directive change. Actually both participation *and* direction are needed. Participative change processes are not effective without clear direction and leadership. Directive approaches are not effective unless those expected to change are fully involved in the process. People who are continually in the midst of change need information and direction more than ever—somebody pointing the way, telling them how to go about doing things. Like most principles that are being applied in these whitewater times, it's a paradox...

Leaders need to be directive about participation.

An important role of the Steering Committee and the organization-wide P Design Team is to manage the balance of direction and participation. In doing this, they must see themselves as true partners of the people in the organization, and act accordingly. Partnering leaders are sensitive to the key concerns people have as they move through change and understand that people going through change need both direction and support, but in varying degrees. At first the need is for leaders to provide more direction—telling people where the change is leading, what needs to be done, and how they can get involved. People want to understand as much about the change as possible. They can't contribute to something they know little about, and if the intent is to have them become involved in and take responsibility for the change process, everybody needs to have the same information. GE's Jack Welch says it well:

How do you bring people into the change process? Start with reality. Get all the facts out. Give people the rationale for change, laying it out in the clearest, most dramatic terms. When everybody gets the same facts, they'll generally come to the same conclusion. Only after everyone agrees on the reality and resistance is lowered can you begin to get buy-in to the needed change.
The rule about ownership is:

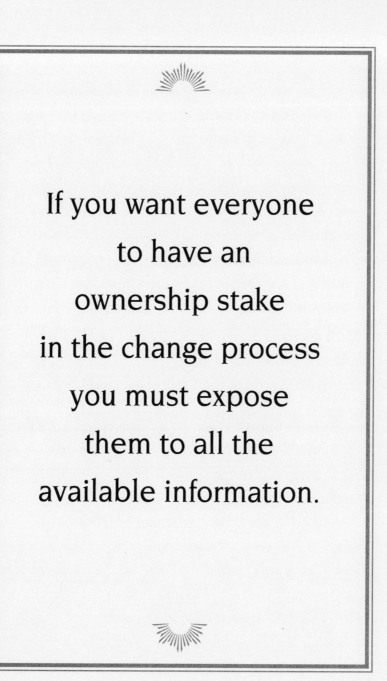

If you want everyone
to have an
ownership stake
in the change process
you must expose
them to all the
available information.

As the change effort gains momentum and people become more comfortable with the change and their involvement, the Steering Committee and the P Design Team do not need to provide as much direction and information. Now their role is more to provide support, encouragement, and inspiration until everyone fully owns the change and has internalized what it takes to make it part of the on-going culture.

In the past the problem with implementing change in organizations has been that most "change agents" (usually top managers) did not stay on track. They announced the desired change, pitched the benefits, maybe answered a few questions, then disappeared—only to seagull in when there was no progress and punish everyone. What is needed is a supportive environment that provides appropriate movement from dependency ("Tell me what's going on.") through involvement ("I feel like a partner in this change effort.") to ownership ("This change is part of me.")

- **An Environment of Support.** In many ways, guiding change effectively is like being a good parent. When the parent of a tot thinks in terms of a prescribed plan (creep by 5 months, crawl by 8 months, walk by a year, talk by a year and a half), the unique needs and characteristics of that particular child can become lost. If the child is seen as "late" in achieving any of these tasks, the parent starts to worry, "What's wrong? Why isn't he as far along as my cousin's kid?" The parent begins to try to hurry the process, communicating to the child that something is wrong and placing stress on the relationship.

Suppose the tot deviates from some behavioral norm in the parent's head, say, demands a drink before going to sleep, or starts throwing food from his highchair. The parent listens to conventional wisdom. ("You can't let him manipulate you. If he gets a drink tonight, he'll want one every night.") Again, the parent may frustrate the normal process of development by placing unnecessary pressure on the relationship or by trying to change or repress the behavior.

An entirely different approach is taken by the parent who sees everything the young child does in terms of a naturally unfolding developmental process. If the child asks for a drink, the parent gives it. If the child throws food, the parent may not like cleaning it up, but he or she says, "He's testing spatial relationships, he's observing cause and effect," or just, "He's having a ball!" In this same vein, the wise parent of a teenager knows that behavior that asserts independence from parental control is to be expected, since this is a developmentally appropriate task. That parent takes steps to see that the behavior occurs within a framework where the teenager can see that she is understood, loved, and supported—and that the need for direction is still operating.

What is the experience of employees who are treated in this way? They know they are dealing with a system that is trying to understand them, in an environment where they can get their needs met. Like children in a family, they may go through rough times and have to endure things they don't like and wouldn't choose on their own, but they are willing to endure because the adults on the scene are not taking their behavior personally, care about them, and are expressing belief in them and their ability to deliver their best in trying times. These employees will be more likely to be loyal and to eventually act to ensure the well-being of their organizational "family."

If people are led through change in this way, there will be at any given time the cooperation of a critical mass of people who have a positive attitude, and who become the ones who carry the organization forward from day to day, and also forward in the change process. Not only do they serve as a support to the leaders of the change, they also provide role models for those who are struggling with the process.

Final Thoughts

While our discussion on the Deliver step only has focused on First Curve improvements, you are likely to encounter the same issues once a decision has been made to implement a Second Curve innovation. Jumping from the First Curve to the Second Curve is all about managing change and closing the gaps between **what is happening now and what you would like to be happening**.

As we end this chapter on First Curve efforts, we want to encourage you to keep these activities in perspective. First Curve work represents only one part of the two-pronged commitment to change. The world-class company is improving its present *while* designing its future. In order to stress the simultaneity of activity of the two curves, the next chapter will be devoted to an outline of Second Curve efforts.

CHAPTER THREE

TAKING THE HIGH GROUND: SECOND-CURVE INNOVATIONS

Leadership is going where no one else has gone.
Bob Galvin, *former chairman of Motorola*

S uppose you choose to participate on an F team. Beyond your "day job" you also will be using your discretionary time to scout the future. What *is* the future? We encourage you to provide that limitless span with your own definition, but for our purposes we define the future as **the period between eighteen months and five years from now.**

In the First Curve you're trying to get people unstuck from their behavior. In the Second Curve you're trying to get people unstuck from the way they think. The tools whose purpose is to continuously improve that which you already have may help to keep your company afloat today, but they do little to prepare you for the market of tomorrow. For that, a whole new set of tools needs to be developed. A very different mindset from First Curve focus needs to be established; it begins by asking the question, "If we didn't exist, would we reinvent ourselves and, if so, what would we look like?"

To get started, you may find it useful to have the organization-wide F Design Team with the help of F Team members ponder the following sets of questions:

F Team Questions

The Customer

- Does it seem likely that you'll be serving the same customers in the future that you are serving today? If not, how will tomorrow's customers be different?
- Through which channels will you reach tomorrow's customers?
- Where will industry lines be drawn in the future?

The Competition

- What will be the basis of competition—continuous innovation, cooperative competition, mass customization, or what?
- What will the competition look like?
- What must we do to ensure that the industry evolves in a way that is to our maximum advantage?

Our Company

- What strategic capabilities must we build to ensure survival, or better yet, market domination? How will we build them?
- What alliances will we need to develop?
- What will be the profile of a typical employee? Will he or she report to the office every morning to work or work from home? What will he or she expect to receive in exchange for time and effort?

In studying these questions and trying to make sense of the answers, the F Teams will be applying the same three steps we used in our First Curve description but with a markedly different twist.

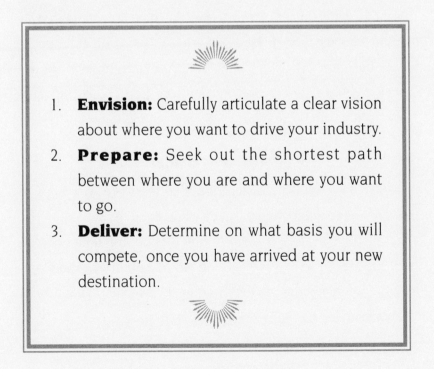

1. **Envision:** Carefully articulate a clear vision about where you want to drive your industry.
2. **Prepare:** Seek out the shortest path between where you are and where you want to go.
3. **Deliver:** Determine on what basis you will compete, once you have arrived at your new destination.

Let's examine each of these steps in more detail as it applies to the unknown future.

ENVISION

We have continually emphasized that a world-class organization is not only constantly improving its present operation but is committed to creating a new competitive space in the future. The corporate-wide F Design Team must generate a shared vision of the future competitive state toward which you are working. What exactly that vision is, only **you** will know. You must come up with your own vision, unique to your kind of business. Yet, no matter where your business sits on the spectrum, the Envision step should begin with a scanning of the horizon, particularly when it comes to Second Curve leadership and technology.

Second-Curve Leadership

George Bernard Shaw once wrote that there are two types of people in the world: the reasonable and the unreasonable. "The reasonable man adapts himself to the world; the unreasonable one persists in trying to adapt the world to himself. Therefore, all progress depends on the unreasonable man." Market innovations are led by unreasonable people.

In creating new opportunities, companies must be capable of leading customers to where they want to go—but don't even know it yet. This is not a new phenomenon in business. For example, Nokia foresaw the trend toward wireless telephony and invested in it early; it is now the number two supplier of cellular telephones in the world. Ted Turner, recognizing that people were working longer and more unpredictable hours and thus could not watch network news at scheduled times, created a cable news network that provided news around-the-clock. *The Miami Herald*, responding to the growing Hispanic population in South Florida, launched a full sister Spanish-language newspaper called *El Nuevo Herald* which has become more profitable than the *Herald* itself.

Opportunity hunting is what Second Curve leaders are all about. They anticipate rather than respond to market demand. They go where few fear to tread. Steve Jobs is a perfect example of this type of market activist (creator/antagonist/pioneer/adventurer). He had been hailed as a visionary when at age 21 he created Apple Computer with Steve Wozniak and later spearheaded development of the Macintosh computer. Then in 1985 he was ejected from the company by John Sculley, whom he had hired as CEO. There followed a decade of anguish and millions of dollars in losses with NeXT, the computer company he founded after leaving Apple. Yet even while he was down, Jobs was not out. As suggested in a December 2, 1995 *USA Today* article entitled "Former Silicon Valley Brat Hits Stride," Steve

Jobs "woke up last Tuesday reborn." Now suddenly Steve Jobs was an instant billionaire with the takeoff of his computer animation company Pixar, which created the hit animated film *Toy Story*.

The Steve Jobs story exemplifies the kind of complete absorption in Second Curve thinking that is required of leaders if they are to orchestrate a breakthrough and lead others into new competitive space. Despite his losses, he continues to focus his energy, charisma, impatience, and drive on the future, and he is good at making people believe that almost anything is possible. Ed McCracken, CEO of Silicon Graphics, has said of Jobs, "If you're not careful when you're with him, you can end up not knowing what's real and what's not."

"Future-tects" like Steve Jobs who set out on a journey of creating the future must begin with a clear picture of what they want to create. Having a vision does not guarantee a profitable journey toward the future; but without one, the journey cannot even begin. Which raises the question: How does one develop a vision? Hamel and Prahalad provide some interesting thoughts on this.

> For a variety of reasons we prefer the word foresight to vision. Vision connotes a dream or an apparition but there is more to industry foresight than a single blinding flash of insight. Industry foresight is based on deep insight into the trends in technology, demographics, regulation and lifestyles that can be harnessed to rewrite industry rules and create

new competitive space. While understanding the potential complication of such trends requires creativity and imagination, any "vision" that is not based on solid factual foundation is likely to be fantastical.

To take their argument one step further, knowledge and imagination do not drive industry revolutions—people do. These drivers must have the courage and tenacity to be contrarians and to stick with it until they have accomplished what they set out to do.

Thus, industry revolution is all about wisdom and courage. The wisdom to ask the right questions, and the courage to answer them—regardless of where those answers may lead us. Today one can't begin to formulate these questions, much less answer them, unless one first takes a look at the enormous impact technology is having upon all of us.

Revolution in Technology

What makes Second Curve thinking so important for organizations is the fact that today's world is in a state of recurring change. At the forefront of this change is a revolution in technology. Almost single-handedly, technology is obliterating the existing industrial model of society. The convergence of telephones, televisions, computers, and consumer electronics seems almost certain to create seismic shifts in the way governments govern, companies compete, and people work and play. The instant availability of information by electronic means is producing profound changes in every arena of human experience.

The political and economic revolution going on all around us is likely to be as profound and as disruptive as that which brought us out of the agrarian age and into the industrial age. Peter Drucker writes:

> Every few hundred years throughout Western history, a sharp transformation has occurred. In a matter of decades, society altogether rearranges itself—its world view, its basic values, its social and political structures, its arts, its key institutions. Fifty years later a new world exists. And the people born into that world cannot even imagine the world in which grandparents lived and into which their own parents were born. ***Our age is such a period of transformation.***

We can see this transformation occurring on a variety of levels: national, corporate, and individual.

National. We are coming to the end of that phase of democracy that we think of as "representative democracy." In his book ***Global Paradox,*** John Naisbitt talks about the "end of politics":

> The crisis in political leadership we are witnessing today is the crisis of an earlier invented arrangement that has become irrelevant. Because we are now in a position to know all we have to know as soon as everyone else knows it—including those who represent us—we do not have to have that kind of ***representativeness*** anymore. We don't have to have people on the scene who have the knowledge and information to make judgments for us. We have the same information and knowledge and we are also on the scene.

Corporate. The technological revolution is having no less an effect on corporations. With everyone having access to the same facts and figures at the same time, decision making no longer remains the exclusive domain of leadership—it becomes a requirement of all. Management becomes a set of tasks and activities, not a layer of insulation or a full-time job title. Everyone manages, although some have a wider view and a longer time perspective.

Likewise, technology is making work *something you do,* rather than *somewhere you go.* People no longer need to show up at the office or factory to do a day's work—they can do it from home, the car, or just about anywhere. The move toward a wireless society is spawning an age of networked entrepreneurs, proving again that *the greater the power of technology, the more empowered and liberated its individual users become.*

Individual. Technology's impact on the homefront is likely to be no less profound. It is turning our private space into a virtual shopping mall. Already we're able to buy airline tickets online, but that is only the beginning. As encryption technology improves to the point where we feel comfortable in sending our credit card numbers zipping out into cyberspace, interactive television is likely to become the marketplace of choice. Whether people want to design and buy their own clothing, play video games against distant opponents, buy groceries, make

83

hotel reservations, watch a movie on demand, or simply catch up on the latest news or reviews, they'll be able to do it all with a few keystrokes and without ever having to leave the couch. People will no longer need to worry about leaving home without their credit cards—they won't need to leave home, period.

But even when they do eventually venture out of their home/work space, people will once again find it impossible to escape the onslaught of new technologies. As an example of this, Bill Gates, CEO of Microsoft, predicts in his book **The Road Ahead** that the wallet as we know it today will cease to exist in a few year's time. It will come to be replaced by what he calls a "wallet PC."

> Rather than holding paper currency, the new wallet will store unforgeable digital money. Your wallet will link into a store's computer to allow money to be transferred without any physical exchange at a cash register. Digital cash will be used in interpersonal transactions, too. If your son needs money, you might digitally slip five bucks from your wallet PC to his.

How soon will all this happen? The likely error these days is on the conservative side—things happen faster, not slower, than expected. As Gates contends:

> A decade ago few of us had ever heard of a cellular phone, a personal pager, or a facsimile machine. Go back a few more years and you can add the Sony Walkman, the compact disc and the hand-held camcorder. Some of us can go

back further still to a time when there were no televisions and no computers.

How, then, will tomorrow's markets look, given that they will be significantly shaped by rapid improvements in technology? Will they closely resemble those of today? It's doubtful. The inescapable conclusion: *If you are not involved today in creating tomorrow's markets, or knowledgable about what's happening in these markets, you are unlikely to find yourself competing in them.*

Peering into the Future

Where will all this futuristic information come from? Foretelling the future, or at least some of its key themes, is not as impossible as it sounds. Our world possesses considerable momentum and continuity. For example, many legislative changes are foreseeable years in advance. Similarly, most demographic shifts can be seen coming a long way off. Even technological advances and their impacts can be predicted to a great extent.

It must also be said that nothing is ever absolutely certain—other than possibly death and taxes. Which means that the old adage, "the road to the future is paved with uncertainty," does have some truth to it. Recognizing these realities, the challenge for managers becomes one of separating those assumptions about the future that you are very confident about from those that remain largely uncertain. Put another way, you need to be able to sort out "predetermined elements" and "uncertainties."

Predetermined events are those that have already occurred or almost certainly will occur, but their consequences have yet to unfold. Uncertainties, on the other hand, are wild cards. They are events no one could have foreseen. Examples could include natural disasters, totally unexpected results of a political election (i.e., the election of the "Olive Tree Party" in Italy), a sudden run on a nation's currency, which in turn precipitates a sudden surge in interest rates with all of its domino effects, and so on.

To deepen your understanding of the differences between "predetermined elements" and "uncertainties" consider the following example: Suppose heavy monsoon rains hit the upper part of the Ganges River basin. With little doubt, forecasters could predict that something extraordinary will happen within two days at Rishikesh in the foothills of the Himalayas; three or four days later in Allahabad; and at Benares, two days after that. They derive this knowledge not by gazing into a crystal ball but by recognizing the future implications of a rainfall that has already occurred or is currently taking place.

There are always elements of the future that are predetermined, but seldom enough of them to permit a single-line forecast that takes account of residual uncertainties. Continuing on the above analogy, though the flood path is predetermined, the extent of the damage it will cause is not. The difficulty in predicting this stems from the uncertainties involved: how much rain will fall, how saturated the marshlands will be along the flood plain when it falls, whether the flood waters will have a chance to recede before the next dousing begins, whether the rains will be accompanied by high winds, etc.

Any sincere attempt to imagine how the future may unfold requires a technique that combines the mystic properties of a crystal ball with the 180-degree perspective of a wide-angle lens. Does such a technique exist? Not really, but by combining two techniques—*scenario planning* and *intuitive thinking*—the desired effect can be achieved.

Scenario Planning

The first of these techniques was originally developed by Herman Kahn but was popularized by Arrie P. DeGeus and other members of the Royal Dutch/Shell strategic planning group. In its simplest terms, scenario planning is a disciplined method for imagining and examining a company's different possible futures. Scenarios are not plans *per se*, they're hypothetical sketches of what the company's future could look like.

To get a feel for the differences between traditional corporate planning and scenario planning, it may be useful to consider another example. In this case, however, we'll leave the Himalayas and head for the Alps. Now suppose for a moment that you're suited up and standing at the base of one of the mountains preparing to begin your assent. Before starting out you take one last look at the map you've brought along with you. Detailed though it may be, your map does little to prepare you for what lies ahead. As a two-dimensional representation of reality, it ignores variable elements such as weather, landslides, wild animals, and other hikers. To overcome these deficiencies you refer to your previous mountaineering experience and consider a limited number of "what if" scenarios. What will you do if you are held up for three days on the last leg of the journey because of severe weather conditions? What will you do if an avalanche forces you to radically alter your planned route to the summit? What if you chance upon a grizzly and her cub? None of these events may occur, but any might.

The most important of these uncertainties is the weather. You could gather detailed meteorological data on the past seasons, perhaps using computer simulations. But scenario planning goes one step further. It simplifies the extensive data into a limited number of possible states. Each scenario tells a story of how various elements could interact under certain conditions. When relationships between elements can be formalized, a company can develop quantitative models. It should evaluate each scenario for internal consistency and plausibility. (For example, **both** experiencing blizzard conditions **and** meeting a couple of grizzlies is an improbable combination of events.) Though a scenario's boundary may appear fuzzy, a detailed and realistic narrative can direct your attention to aspects you would otherwise overlook. (For example, a vivid snowstorm scenario may highlight the need to bring along skin protection, goggles, extra food supplies, a short-wave radio, etc.)

Because scenario planning stimulates decision makers to consider different *possible* future states, it can be a powerful tool for breaking through traditional thinking and undercutting the prevailing mindsets. "What would it take to get our costs down by 30 percent?" Radical questions such as that one can be answered only through out-of-the-box thinking. (If it isn't radical enough try 50 percent!)

Scenario planning attempts to capture the richness and range of possibilities, opening the eyes of all those involved in the exercise to those opportunities and threats they might otherwise have ignored. We've talked about scenario planning in mountain climbing; now let's apply it to your corporate world.

The Scenario Planning Process

Suppose you select members from various F Teams to participate with the F Design Team in a scenario planning process. The process should consist of the following steps:

1. ***Develop a Common Understanding.*** Scenario planning is a complex and time-consuming process, one that involves all layers of management. Each new participant should be made to understand what scenario planning is, and why it is useful.

2. ***Define the Scope.*** Define the time frame and scope of the scenario, and which served markets, customer groups, technologies, and types of competitors will be included. Consider factors such as where you think you are on your First Curve;

the impact that technology is having in shaping the industry; the current rate of technological change; the ease with which foreign competitors can penetrate your core markets; the aggressiveness, tenacity, and flexibility of your current and anticipated competitors; and your organization's current and forecasted state of financial health. Which other specific issues you should include in the analysis will vary from situation to situation.

3. ***Identify Major Trends.*** Identify the political, economic, societal, technological, legal, and industry trends that affect, or are likely to affect, the issues you have identified. To gain a detailed and comprehensive understanding of the trends shaping your market calls for boundless curiosity and a willingness to explore and follow out each branching set of findings.

Don't expect to complete this work in hours or days; think rather in terms of weeks and months. Because of the multiplicity of trends that need to be considered in conducting this effort, you might want to look outside your F teams for additional participants to ensure that those involved in the process are an eclectic mix of insiders and outsiders (suppliers, customers, consultants, academics, regulators). It isn't unusual to have 20 or more people; some groups have exceeded 200. Your group of trend-watchers should begin by developing a list of trends that are already at work in the industry and have the potential to profoundly upset the status quo. Each of these trends should then be examined in greater detail.

4. ***Identify Key Uncertainties.*** While many trends can simply be

rolled forward, not all trends fall into this category. Some events and outcomes that will inevitably affect the issues you are concerned with cannot be predicted. Will a new technology suddenly appear out of some obscure research laboratory no one has ever heard of? Will a major political event result in the passage of a totally unexpected piece of legislation? Accept uncertainty; try to understand it and make it a part of your reasoning process. List key uncertainties, and attach possible outcomes. To keep from getting bogged down in fruitless debate, keep these outcomes simple and limited in number. It may be difficult to deal with these uncertainties, but ignoring them in the hope that they will never develop simply won't do.

5. ***Construct Initial Scenario Themes.*** You now have enough guidelines to begin constructing your first-generation scenarios. A scenario essentially is a story that describes, in as much detail as possible, one way in which its creators think the future may unfold. Each scenario should describe a different world rather than different outcomes in the same world. The term "first generation" indicates an ongoing process. The first round typically does not produce images clear and compelling enough to be used in decision making. That's the goal of the second round of the process. The goal of the first round is to gain a deeper understanding of the mechanics of the business environment: what forces are at work, how they interact, what is predetermined and what is not, and so on.

   Ask each team of scenario writers to weave its story around a special set of circumstances. For instance, one scenario (the "surprise-free" scenario) might be based upon a continuation of the present. A second might include all the worst possible events that could take place. A third could explore a utopian state of affairs. In developing these different storylines, equal doses of prediction and imagination should be injected into the process. Remember, the primary purpose of constructing these models of the future is not to try to produce scenarios which will later be found to mirror reality, but rather to try to gain a deeper understanding of the forces at work within your industry.

Experts tell us that in constructing scenarios the ideal is to create "one plus two," the surprise-free view (showing explicitly why and where it is fragile), plus two other worlds that focus on completely different sets of circumstances. "One plus two plus one" might be an even more useful formula. In applying this method you would first use the surprise-free scenario to poke holes in your current assumption base (challenge First Curve thinking). The next two scenarios would begin with **what is** and overlay it with two different sets of possibilities, deliberately set at opposite ends of the spectrum. The final scenario would take a stab at Second Curve imagineering. It would begin with **what could** be and work back to what must happen if that future is to come about.

6. ***Initiate Institutional Learning.*** The simple worlds you have just constructed are probably not yet full-fledged scenarios, because they contain inconsistencies and uncertainties. To eliminate these deficiencies involve others in the process. The

more minds you apply to any given problem, the greater the likelihood that a satisfactory solution will be found. Include as many people as possible, especially some from P teams. The more connected your people feel to a process, the more likely it is they will support its results. Share the partially completed scenarios with managers from all over the company. Ask them to identify obvious inconsistencies, then consider how they would respond to each of these different worlds. Adding to strategic ideas and possibilities that had previously been beyond their reach will obligate managers to question their own model of reality, and to change it as necessary.

7. **Construct Final Decision Scenarios.** The teams now return to the drawing board to hammer out a final set of scenarios that can be used by executives in making decisions. Since the goal of the scenarios is to quantify key variables relating to each of the different worlds, the teams need to think through the implications and consequences of each. Each scenario poses a different set of strategic challenges and requisite core competencies. These must be identified and fully explored.

8. **Make a Decision.** With each of the different scenarios laid out before them, participants in the scenario planning process (most probably the F Design Team) would make a presentation to the Steering Committee. The Steering Committee must decide for itself whether to gamble the future on one scenario, stay flexible enough to exploit multiple scenarios, develop contingency plans in case things go sour, or hedge the risk through strategic planning.

As you grapple with these issues, ask "Are we talking **evolution or revolution?**" Based on our newly developed insights into what lies around the bend, do we now feel that our company's need for change is less or greater than we had previously believed? Our hunch is that for most organizations the answer will be "greater than."

Intuitive Thinking

Scenario planning is a step-by-step process that will help you to peer into the future. To do it properly you will need a facilitator. The second technique, intuitive thinking, is something that is available to every participant in the business world, whether he or she is a top manager or front-line employee. It does not require a facilitator—just trust in yourself. As Nancy Rosanoff, author of **Intuition Workout: A Practical Guide to Discovering and Developing Your Inner Knowing,** writes: "Intuition is when we know, but we don't know how we know." These are times that call for the development of that "sixth sense" all of us have, the ability to generate hunches, to tune in to the knowledge we already possess. The ancient Chinese philosopher Lao-Tzu said, "How do I know the ways of all things at the beginning? By what is within me."

Intuition, however, should in no way be considered a substitute for thinking, being responsible, or gathering all relevant information before making decisions. Intuiting should be considered a **sure** way of knowing things, but we must then determine **how** we know them. Like a little-used muscle, intuition can be trained and become stronger as a result. Ms. Rosanoff says that intuition speaks to us through (1) images and symbols, (2) feelings and emotions, and (3) physical sensations. Each of us has a primary "style" of intuiting: mental, emotional, or kinesthetic. If you are kinesthetic, you will physically feel where your intuition is. If you are mental, it will probably seem like you are making it all up. If you are an emotional/feeling type, intuition will feel real. Also there are often combinations of these intuitive types.

These are days in which paradox rules. That means that the development of intuition is important simply because there are so many things in today's world that cannot be figured out on a rational basis. It may be difficult for the busy executive to find time for solitude and tuning in to his/her inner knowing, and that is to be expected. But as with anything else of importance, you must **make time** for it. A quotation from Rainer Maria Rilke highlights the wisdom that can be gained by regularly going within, away from the noise and strife:

> Be patient toward all that is unsolved in your heart and try to love the questions themselves....Do not now seek the answers which cannot be given you because you would not be able to live them and the point is to **live** everything. Live the questions now. Perhaps you will then gradually, without noticing it, live along some distant day into the answer.

Strategic Ambition

What new and profound customer benefits will you have to offer to ensure yourself a place in that world of the future? What can you offer tomorrow's customers that they will value and be unable to get from anyone else? As your picture of the future begins to come into focus, you will need to figure out where and how your firm can fit into it. Out of this inquiry should come a new **strategic ambition**—a succinct and compelling summation of what you want your company to become.

A strategic ambition is analogous to a personal career ambition. As a person grows up, he or she decides on a career—doctor, lawyer, accountant, mother, and so on. In youth this ambition may be somewhat vague and unsettled, but for most of us maturity brings a clearer understanding of what we want to do with our God-given talents. This then becomes our life's ambition, and all key decisions are made with that overarching goal in mind.

As companies struggle to build their Second Curve, they must make a similar commitment. Walt Disney did this when in the 1960s he dreamed of creating a magical theme park where families could come to have a fun, safe, educational time. Likewise, Henry Ford dreamed of providing a car for every family. These inspiring ambitions haunted their every thought and drove them to accomplish the seemingly impossible, by leaping over or even disregarding obstacles they found in their path. Each of these corporate ambitions was as unique as it was inspiring. Each was based upon *an **intense and unwavering commitment to making a difference in people's lives***.

The challenge facing you now is to craft your own strategic ambition, just as these exemplary leaders did, and then to begin moving toward it. This brings us to the second of the three steps involved in creating new competitive space: developing the competencies and technologies you will need if you are to both shape and profit from the future.

PREPARE

I f the first stage of your second-curve "future-tects" work is to outthink the competition by dreaming of new areas of opportunity, the second stage is to outmaneuver them by shaping the evolution of these developments to your own advantage. To do this, your company must identify the gaps between its current competitive strengths and tomorrow's competitive requirements. Once these have been identified, the next step is to determine how each will be closed. Will you develop the needed skills and technologies on your own? Will you do it through collaboration with others? Or will you do a little of both?

Most companies choose the last approach, as they soon discover that they can't create the future single-handedly. Having made this determination, they then find themselves facing numerous new challenges and questions. For instance, what is the precise nature of each gap in terms of professional expertise? Which gaps are we capable of filling on our own? Which require the assistance of others? How should the acquiring of competencies be managed, and who should manage it?

Let's begin with the issue of internal competence development, then move on to the complex yet alluring world of alliance building—a world with which many are acquainted, but in which few are skilled.

Building New Core Competencies

As we discussed in Chapter 2, core competencies are the skills and technologies unique to an organization. Developing one's core competencies to the point where they become "best in class" is not easily achieved. It can take years to accomplish this feat, and this requires stoic commitment, Herculean effort, and unvarying nerve. Building new core competencies requires management to adopt a whole new perspective on how it manages its future. Rather than leaving things to happenstance, and/or to more fleet-footed competitors, the company is forced to take a more proactive role in creating its own future. This begins with a deep and profound understanding of the differences between today's customers and those the company are likely to be serving in the years ahead. This is followed by a detailed examination aimed at unearthing the core competen-

cies that currently underlie the company's competitive performance. This identification process can take months. As Hamel
and Prahalad warn:

> A substantial amount of effort is required to fully disentangle
> competencies from the products and services in which they
> are embedded, to distinguish core from non-core, to cluster
> and aggregate the skills and technologies in some meaning-
> ful way, and to arrive at "labels" that are truly descriptive
> and promote shared understanding.

Once the existing core competencies have been identified,
the complexity of the task intensifies somewhat in Second
Curve work as the focus shifts from today's known world to that
of tomorrow's uncertain world. Two key questions arise:

1. What new skills and technologies must we develop or
   acquire in order to get to the future first?
2. Which of these core skills and technologies should we develop internally, and which should we acquire externally?

When these two lists have been drawn up, one indicating
your present competencies and the other those you will need to
compete in the future—the task is to strategize how each can
be realized. It is wise to make a single executive fully responsible for the development or acquisition of each of the new competencies. Regular "competence review" meetings should be
held to discuss progress made, further investments required, the
performance and behavior of alliance partners, and plans for

the further strengthening of efforts made to date. This systematic approach will help you to avoid some of the typical dysfunctional organizational behavior in this area: throwing money at a project, scrapping it when it doesn't yield immediate results, jump-starting it again when competition seems to be edging ahead, and then nuking it when a key leadership position changes hands. Such are the ebbs and flows of all too many competence-building initiatives, and such are the reasons why so many of them never make it out of the starting gate.

Reasons to Partner Up

Because of the costs and risks inherent in building world leadership in a core competence area, few companies seem anxious to go it alone. Most find it necessary to join forces with others who offer critical complementary resources. This means forging new strategic alliances.

Business networks are not new, but their proliferation and visibility have increased dramatically in recent years. Some reasons for this are:

- *Globalization.* Strategic alliances are being created daily as part of the process of moving toward a single-market world in which capital, people, and ideas are able to flow effortlessly across borders. Time and distance are unimportant; companies must regard distant aggressors as they always have—local competitors. Even small companies must be world-ready, regardless of whether they have any intention of being world-active. Small firms need to forge alliances in order to extend their reach and achieve the same benefits of scale as their larger competitors. Big companies need to add muscle without adding bulk, which can only be achieved by networking with others.

- **Sharing the Risks.** Strategic alliances are especially prominent at business frontiers where there are new opportunities but also great uncertainties—for example, at the crossroads of information and entertainment (info-tainment); where fossil fuels are giving way to renewable resources such as sun, wind, and sea power; or where Western capitalist thinking bumps up against staunch Communist ideologies in emerging markets such as China and Russia. In each of these opportunity areas the potential rewards are great. So are the risks—which is why few dare to face them alone.

- **Filling the Gaps.** Another factor favoring the formation of alliance groups is the growing complexity not only of products and services but also of their design, production, and delivery. Few companies are able to master all of the requisite skills on their own. Most prefer to focus more narrowly on their own unique sets of core competencies, and then to use their positions of strength to network with others who have the competencies and resources they lack. Each company within these virtual organizations, regardless of size or reputation, is treated as an equal, respected and appreciated for the unique talents it has to offer.

- **Organizational Learning.** Network membership makes learning indispensable. Asian companies in general, and Japanese companies in particular, have been very adept at importing the concepts and competencies of their Western allies, but this isn't a one-way street. Shoichiro Irimarjiri of Honda says: "Joint ventures helped Japanese automakers learn how to operate in the individualistic culture of the U.S., while their U.S. partners learned much about our 'lean production' techniques."

- **Establishing New Technical Standards.** A key reason behind the formation of many alliances (particularly those involving more than two parties) is the need to influence the development of new technical standards. In emerging industries, where a common standard has yet to be established, there can be fierce competition to make one company's particular technical approach the one that ultimately becomes the dominant standard. The winning standard often determines who makes money from the future and who doesn't.

Range of Possibilities

There are many different ways in which alliances can be forged, ranging from temporary and weak to long-term and strong. At one end of the spectrum are **networks** of individuals and/or firms who come together to complete a single task or project and then return from whence they came. At the mid-range are **joint ventures** that formally link companies in pursuit of a single opportunity. At the other end are **partnerships** in which the different parties involved commit to face the future together.

Forming alliances is a more complex process than deciding which type of structure to form. Many companies feel the need to simultaneously participate in many kinds of relationships while playing a different role in each. Let's look at this relationship-building process.

Coming Together

Some words of wisdom from author and consultant Rosabeth Moss Kanter:

> Relationships between companies begin, grow, and develop—or fail—in ways similar to relationships between people. No two relationships travel the same path, but successful alliances generally unfold in five overlapping phases. In the first, courtship, two companies meet, are attracted, and discover their compatibility. During the second—engagement—they draw up plans and close the deal. In phase three, the newly partnered companies, like couples setting up housekeeping, discover they have different ideas about how the business should operate. In phase four, the partners devise mechanisms for bridging those differences and develop techniques for getting along. And in phase five, as old-marrieds, each company discovers that it has changed internally as a result of its accommodations to the ongoing collaboration.

Staying Together

Few alliances make it through all five phases. The honeymoon phase can be bliss, but often within a year or so the participants' troubles begin. It can be disturbingly similar to the failing marriage—squabbles about money, incompatibility, and infidelity. Consider the results Joel Bleeke and David Ernst found in two studies of corporate alliances. The first study found that about two-thirds of alliances run into serious managerial or financial difficulty within two years of their formation. The second found that "the median life span for alliances is only about seven years, and that nearly 80 percent of joint ventures—one of the most common alliance structures—ultimately end in a sale by one of the partners." This research illustrates that most of us are still on a very steep learning curve when it comes to knowing how to successfully partner with one another.

DELIVER

The challenges you face, once you've developed something that customers don't yet know they need, can be formidable. When it comes to positioning a product that no one has ever seen or heard of before, who's to say what will work and what won't? Marketing experts won't know, because they won't have formally studied the subject.

Customers won't be able to provide many insights as they probably won't yet understand or appreciate what you're talking about. Competitors, if they happen to know something, will not be keen to talk about it. This leaves you in a bit of a quandary. How can you set the four P's of marketing—price, product, promotion, and place—when you have little-to-no information or experience to draw upon? We suggest a combination of a pair of strategies—one mental and apparently impractical, the other behavioral and eminently practical.

Reality Creation and Expeditionary Marketing

The ability to create a new reality is a characteristic of visionaries. Walt Disney called this characteristic "imagineering" and found that people who had it thought "outside the box." These people are invaluable because they can see so clearly things that never were, but could be, that they can convince others of their possibility. That is what **reality creation** is all about. This is one of the two critical strategies needed by F Teams in the Deliver stage of the Second Curve operations. These people must become experts at suspending disbelief in themselves and others so that the alternate reality they see is almost tangible. Then they can receive and use feedback from co-workers, customers, and suppliers. At the same time, they must be practical pioneers, using the test-marketing strategy discussed below.

The second key strategy in their arsenal, **expeditionary marketing,** is designed to provide answers to such questions as:

How will we position our new product or service? What design features will customers be interested in? What price points will they find acceptable? What promotional tactics should be used? Which distribution channels would work best? Answers to these questions can only come from the marketplace itself. By making a series of controlled, low-cost incursions into the market, a company can learn where the heart of a future demand actually lies.

It was Hamel and Prahalad that called this type of prospecting "expeditionary marketing." They compare test marketing to an archer shooting at a target through a blanket of fog. The archer could wait for the fog to clear or he could shoot arrows through the fog, using feedback from a forward observer to adjust his aim until he finally hears "Bull's-eye!" The authors contend:

> What counts most in expeditionary marketing is not hitting a bull's eye the first time, but how quickly one can improve one's aim and get another arrow on the way to the target. Little is learned in the laboratory or product development committee meetings. True learning only begins where a product or service—imperfect as it may be—is launched into the market...when it comes to expeditionary marketing, the rules are very simple: Learn faster, learn cheaper.

This approach works best in an atmosphere where failure is viewed as a learning experience.

In the past, market pioneers would expose a new product to

potential customer groups, and ask for their feedback, only after they had tested it to death. Nowadays this approach won't wash. Development costs are too high and product life cycles too short to allow companies to innovate successfully in this way. With the technology available today, companies have the opportunity of inviting customers into the development cycle. Each expeditionary marketing initiative can and should be a joint effort between the company and its targeted customers. With continuous two-way dialogue between these two groups throughout both the product and the subsequent market development process, these technologies can be utilized to their fullest potential to enroll tens if not hundreds of thousands of customers into the process. This way the company is able to create a loyal captive market and cut the time it takes to unlock the mass market.

The success of **The One-Minute Manager,** co-authored by Ken Blanchard and Spencer Johnson, is a perfect example of this strategy. This book was considered innovative for a management book in that it was small (only 102 pages), expensive ($15.00 a copy), and written in the form of a modern-day parable.

As a successful writer of children's books, Johnson had developed an unusual strategy for writing. He wrote the first draft of his books alone, then used frequent interactions with customers to do his rewriting. For example, in writing the **Value of A Sense of Humor: The Story of Will Rogers,** he thought he had written a very funny book. When teachers permitted him to read it to their elementary classes, the kids were bored. They didn't think it was funny, until Johnson mentioned that one day Will's lariat got out of control and he lassoed a teacher. The kids thought this was the funniest thing they'd ever heard. So Johnson went back and wrote more lassoing of teachers into the new version. When he took the revision back to school, the children thought it was a great book. It was now ready for publication.

This is essentially what Blanchard and Johnson did with **The One-Minute Manager.** After writing the first draft, they gave it to hundreds of managers to read and asked them to provide feedback. For example, in a seminar they conducted for Burger King franchisees, these managers zeroed in on the One-Minute Manager's tendency to physically touch people as part of the praising and reprimand process—i.e., a handshake or a pat on the back. The group's comment was, "We're having enough trouble getting the hamburgers out now without our managers touching employees." But the authors thought it was an important concept. They asked how it could be rewritten so that people wouldn't think, "Here come a couple of guys from California selling the 'I-touch-you' method at work." The feedback from the Burger King group was invaluable, and had opened their thinking enough to respond eagerly to an article they came across that Dr. Charles McCormick had written entitled, "If You Touch, Don't Take." His argument was if you touch someone to support and encourage them, they will know that and appreciate it; but if you're touching them to get something back or manipulate them, they will know that, too, and resent it. By including this point in their book, the authors never met with any criticism of their thoughts on touching.

To test the final version one more time, Blanchard and Johnson decided to self-publish the book before going national. Through the efforts of the authors and Blanchard Training and Development, nearly 20,000 books were sold in nine months without any advertising. With tremendous support for the self-published version from corporate leaders of companies such as Lockheed, Seven-Eleven, and Holiday Inns, devotees already were in place when the book was published nationally in the fall of 1982. Ten days after it was released, it was on **The New York Times** best-seller list, and it remained there for almost three years. Over seven million copies have been sold worldwide. Today, small but expensive management books in parable form are commonplace.

By making a number of limited incursions into the market, a company is able to move rapidly forward without putting itself at risk. By viewing failures as learning opportunities, the company encourages risk-taking and entrepreneurism. These are key attributes of companies anxious to create that which does not exist, and to venture where none have ventured before.

The Organization of the Future

Once you determine what kind of business you want to be in down the road, you need to organize yourself to deliver your new product(s) or service(s). What will the organization of the future be like? While there is no way to completely know, we offer the following image as our best guess of what the organization of the future might look like:

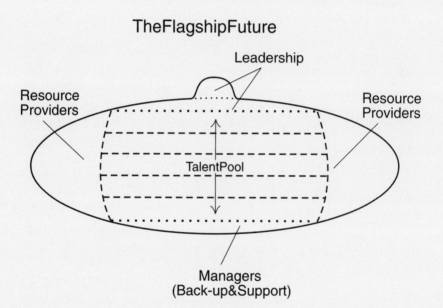

TheFlagshipFuture

Leadership

Resource Providers

Resource Providers

TalentPool

Managers
(Back-up&Support)

As you can tell by the title, our diagram of the new organization is forward looking. In fact, it resembles a spaceship (flying saucer) in which four different groups may be seen operating:

1. Those who provide **leadership** (the people who used to be at headquarters)
2. Those who provide **talent** (we used to call them "employees")
3. Those who provide **resources** (i.e., money, technology, knowledge, personnel)
4. Those who provide **backup and support** (we used to call them "bosses")

The spaceship model is not to be viewed as a vertical hierarchy. For example, the managers (the disappearing bosses) are below the workers, suggesting that they are there to support them and provide them with resources. The lines that indicate the tiers of talent pool members and the domains of resource providers are broken, suggesting that these groups are separated only by semipermeable membranes; people, ideas, and resources flow freely back and forth. To see how each of these different groups may be operating in the future, let's take an imaginary tour through the spaceship.

Leadership

We begin our tour at the top of the flying saucer on the bridge. This is a much smaller area than the old corporate headquarters, for in order to create raving fan customers and ensure financial success, organizations have had to develop committed and empowered employees who are essentially self-managing. The corporate Steering Committee is having a session in the meeting room. It is busy analyzing data recently submitted from the P and F Design Teams and coordinating efforts to keep the ship on its present course while anticipating any dramatic weather changes that may occur farther ahead on their trip. There are relatively few people here, for the bridge is a place where leaders hang their hats but don't spend much time. In fact the captain has told us, "My office is where my mail arrives before it's faxed to me wherever I might be, inside or outside the ship."

If the leaders aren't here, where are they and what are they doing? They are spreading the vision throughout the ship. While the big picture and direction for the ship starts here the vision has to be owned by everyone. Once the vision has been agreed upon, the role of the wandering leaders is to do three things—communicate, communicate, and communicate!—until every single person understands the vision and the entire crew is living it.

As we move about the ship we find the leaders constantly on the move, striving to "walk their talk" by serving as living symbols of the desired corporate culture. While they must set demanding standards, they are constantly encouraging people and helping them believe that established goals can be accomplished. In the process leaders are resolving conflicts by means of a problem-solving rather than a blaming approach. Indeed, as we tour the spaceship we note a sign in one passage that delights us. It reads:

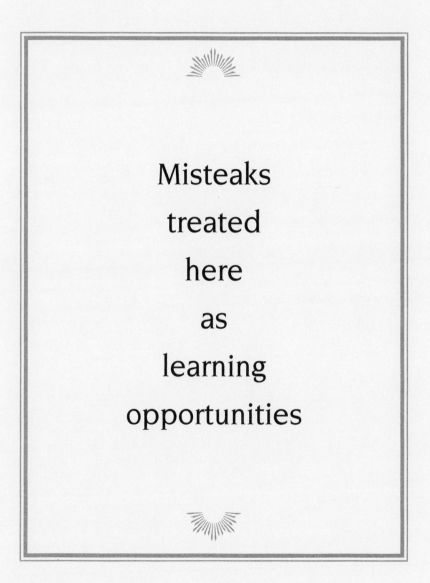

Misteaks

treated

here

as

learning

opportunities

Everywhere we go we notice that leadership is making sure the old hierarchy doesn't sneak back into place so that when people say, "Aye, aye, captain" what they really mean is, "No way that will happen." We discover that leaders spend a good amount of time away from the ship, building relationships with customers, suppliers, and strategic alliances. They know that business today is a relationships game.

The Talent Pool

As we wander about the ship, we see rank and file people who clearly have been thoroughly trained and empowered and are in charge. They go about their duties as owners, making decisions and solving problems in the best interest of all. The pride emanating from crew members is in notable contrast to the days when employees felt like second-class citizens who had been asked to leave their brains at home.

What we find amazing is that these folks can have this kind of commitment in a workplace that provides no guarantees. When we query one crew member about this, he tells us, "These days you have a better chance of getting a gold watch from a street vendor than from your company."

When we ask him if that makes him insecure, he says, "'Anxious,' is a better word, but I'm feeling much better now that I have this!" He gestures with a thick file folder. "It's my portfolio. It shows what I can do. There are letters from supervisors, co-workers on projects, and customers who have said that

I helped to make them raving fans of our company. I'm always upgrading my skills. Using my portfolio, I market myself within the company when new projects are announced where I think I can make a contribution and also increase my chances in the labor market, if that's ever necessary."

We ask him what he expects from the organization. He smiles and says, " A worthwhile mission, good colleagues that are honest with me and challenge me to do my best, and practical training that prepares me to respond to the demands of both internal and external customers in a helpful manner. These kinds of experiences will continue to add to my capabilities. They'll also make me want to stay on here."

Resource Providers

The resource provider group is made up of staff teams that reside on the periphery, amidships, where people can move in any direction when called upon to help. They operate much differently than the legal, finance, accounting, human resource, and personnel departments of old, who saw themselves simply as an extension of top management.

One accounting officer smiles as she tells us, "We used to think senior management set the policy and our job was to implement it. We served as the eyes, ears, and voice of senior management. It used to be pretty grim, trying to catch people doing things wrong, and controlling, policing, and auditing their activities. Today we're here to offer advice and support to work teams whenever we're called upon. We add value to our customers."

When we ask who her customers are, she is quick to reply. "Anyone within the organization who needs my help. I see myself not as a parent chastising children, but as a partner whose role is to educate and support. How well I perform in that role will impact my pay."

"Your pay?" we ask.

"Sure," she nods. "In the past, we were considered part of overhead charges, and the people who used our services had no role in setting our fee. They were stuck with us, even if they could find a more efficient and cost-effective vendor outside the organization. Nowadays those outside folks are our competition. We could end up being outsourced. We get paid, and are billed to a department, only if we are seen as being helpful."

We next speak with a personnel officer, and learn that his department is able to offer its services outside the organization "We're all entrepreneurs here" he tells us, "marketing our services inside and outside the organization. Rather than draining energy from the ship, we hope we add fuel to everyone's activities."

Backup and Support

Down in the hold of the ship are the managers, the people who were once thought of as bosses. From below, they cheerfully offer support to the crews in the engine room and elsewhere. We sit down with one energetic manager and ask him about his change of scene. "Sometimes I'm a banker," he says. "In this role I secure funds for projects, and advise people about what results are needed to ensure future financial support. At other times I'm a broker or talent agent, supplying teams with the people, products, and training they need. When disagreements come up I sometimes play the part of facilitator, helping settle conflicts and resolve decision deadlocks. My survival depends on my ability to provide value to my customers—our work teams."

By taking you on this journey through an imaginary space-ship, we are not trying to do the work of your F Teams. This picture of a future organization is simply our way of saying that tomorrow's organizations are certain to look very different than today's seem. In fact, there will probably be no "typical" struc-ture at all, but a great variety of structures, depending on the unique competitive situation of each company. It is also impor-tant to note that change will occur not only in the areas of structure but will include the redesign of business processes, the revamping or upgrading of systems, the development of new skills, and changes in the organization's culture. Everything has to be adapted to changes in the environment.

Final Thoughts

Earlier we said any sincere attempt to imagine how the future will unfold (which is what Second Curve thinking is all about) requires a technique that combines the mystic properties of a crystal ball with the 180-degree perspective of a wide-angle lens. While such a technique does not exist, by asking F Teams throughout the organization to think, read, and contemplate the future, the desired effect can be achieved. Add the focusing power of the organizationwide F Design Team, and you've got a powerful telescope with which to gaze into the company's future.

By treating the First Curve and Second Curve teams separately in this book, we by no means are implying that they are to be like two separate companies that have nothing to do with each other. In fact they cannot be effective unless they are operating in synch with each other. The world-class company is designing its future *while* improving its present. In the next chapter we will consider ways in which the two curves may be harmonized so as to ensure world-class status.

CHAPTER FOUR

PUTTING THE
RIGHT PEOPLE
ON THE RIGHT TEAM
WITH THE RIGHT KIND
OF SUPPORT

Cultural flexibility is the mental habit of overlooking superficial differences in physical appearance, personal beliefs, dietary preferences, and lifestyles to find a basis for mutual respect and communication.

Thomas S. Watson, Jr., **Connecting People: Discovering Peace and Power through Cultural Flexibility**

S uppose a scout is exploring the terrain ahead of an advancing group of pioneers when he comes unexpectedly upon the encampment of a large hostile tribe. Four scenarios could occur out of this situation.

1. The scout senses the danger, yet decides to let the pioneers fend for themselves because of his strong dislike of their leader and some of the people, and rides off in a different direction.
2. The scout rides quickly back to the leader to report the danger, but the leader, lacking respect for the scout, does not believe his report and takes no defensive action.
3. The leader believes the scout's report, but is unable to organize his people in time to take appropriate action.
4. The leader believes the scout and is able to seize the moment, quickly mobilize his group, and reroute the exploring party to avoid trouble.

Only the fourth scenario makes any sense. Note that it depends on mutual respect, clear communication, and skill on the part of both leader and scout. Both of them need to have subjugated their egos to the higher purpose of shared success.

We use this example to emphasize the importance of effectively integrating the activities of both First Curve and Second Curve thinkers in your organization. This is easier said than done because First Curve thinkers and Second Curve thinkers are like two very different cultures who are required to live and work in harmony. In asking people in aspiring world-class organizations to choose their transformational job from two alternatives (a P or an F team), we recognized these differences. While it might make sense to differentiate them for their initial work, eventually they will have to work together if they are to attain world-class status.

BRAIN MODES

One way to think about the difference between First and Second Curve thinkers is in terms of the classic distinctions between the left and right hemispheres of the brain. (Although we realize that these days discussion centers more around whole-brain thinking, we have chosen the familiar left-brain/right-brain dichotomy simply for the purpose of illustrating our point.)

Everyone uses both sides of the brain, but each side serves a different function. While some people have a good mix of both sides, most depend more on one side of the brain than the other in their day-to-day living. People who are thought of as right-brain thinkers tend to be more intuitive and creative, while left-brain people are more logical and rational. As a result, their thought sequencing is quite different.

For a right-brain thinker that sequence is:

Feeling ⟶ Action ⟶ Analysis

Right-brain thinkers will feel or sense that something is right to do and take action on it. Only after they've done so will they stop to analyze the pros and cons.

The left-brain thought sequence is the exact reverse of that of the right-brain thinker:

Analysis ⟶ Action ⟶ Feeling

According to Dorothy Lehmkuhl and Dolores Cotter Lamping, co-authors of **Organizing for the Creative Person,** before a left-brain person will take action on anything:

> ...they'll analyze the pros and cons (sometimes to death). If the idea is deemed logical or practical, they'll consider all the consequences, plan, and perhaps even talk themselves out of doing it before even getting started! Only when action is completed, however, will they appreciate the feelings gained from it.

Some people, when they learn about the characteristics of left- and right-brain thinkers, tend to grin and gloat, thinking to themselves how *they* certainly wouldn't want to live like their hemispheric counterparts. Yet to put together a world-class organization, both kinds of thinkers are needed. Without the strengths and characteristics of each, the effort to combine present and future concerns will fail. In the past, left- and right-brain (e.g., First Curve and Second Curve) thinkers have not easily found ways to coexist. The Apple Computer story about Steve Jobs' relationship with John Sculley is an illustration of this phenomenon.

Sculley was brought in as the professional manager to do what he'd done at PepsiCo—create a more efficient, better-running First Curve operation. As Apple prospered it outgrew its informal entrepreneurial way of doing business—its lack of systems and clear strategy could no longer be tolerated. Life needed to be pumped into the present operation, or competition would have soon overtaken Apple. Initially, Jobs and Sculley were soul mates; they admired and respected each other. But then they began to second-guess and play in each other's sand-boxes. Jobs started to criticize some of the necessary organizational improvements that were being made; Sculley began to lose confidence in Jobs' vision of the future. A showdown developed; the board chose to back John Sculley, and Steve Jobs left Apple.

Doubtless some difficulties will arise from the attempt to combine the efforts of a First Curve specialist and a Second Curve visionary. But when you can manage it, the marriage of these two kinds of thinking can send your company right off the map. For example, most insiders at Disney feel it wasn't just Michael Eisner who catapulted them into the future, but it was the respect and working relationship between Eisner and his President and COO, Frank Wells. While Eisner seemed to have a crystal ball about where Disney needed to go and the businesses it needed to be in, Wells continually redesigned their systems to embrace these new directions. (It's interesting to note that prior to the Eisner-Wells era, Disney was in serious trouble; it lacked the Second Curve thinking that Walt had embodied and was betting its future on pursuing perfection in existing served markets. It has only been in recent years that it has leveraged its brand name by aggressively moving into the retail, software, film and theater industries.)

We're talking here about a very special relationship, with a very special job to do—creating the future while managing the present. When you begin to understand the possibilities inherent within the partnering of left-brain strategists and right-brain visionaries, you wonder at how organizations ever got along with just one kind. It's equivalent to having to function with only half a brain. While descriptions of left-brain and right-brain thinking are interesting and useful, management consultant and author Ichak Adizes takes the balancing issue one step further.

DIFFERENT FUNCTIONS

Focusing on the different functions that people serve, Adizes says there are four managerial roles that must be performed if an organization is to be run effectively: *producing, implementing, innovating,* and *integrating.*

PRODUCING

Every organization needs people who can get jobs done. Good **producers** have extensive technical skills in their field, whether it be sales, engineering, accounting, or whatever.

IMPLEMENTING

Organizations also need **administrators** who are good at implementing goals. They know how to plan, organize, coordinate and control work.

INNOVATING

Another need in organizations is innovation. **Entrepreneurs** are people who can look into the future, sense what is to be done, and communicate it to others.

INTEGRATING

For organizations to be effective, they need people who can motivate and mobilize people. **Integrators** can take an individual goal and make it a group goal.

These four roles set up the demand side of the management equation. This side of the equation represents the needs of the organization. There is also a supply side of the equation. It relates to what people bring to the management party. People bring skills but they also bring a style of thinking and acting. In fact, Adizes postulates that there are four basic management styles or personalities. Each style has characteristic thought and behavior patterns that make them consistent with one critical role. **Producers** (P) are good at making things happen. **Administrators** (A) are good at creating and maintaining order. **Entrepreneurs** (E) are good at innovating, and **Integrators** (I) are good at building teamwork. The challenge in organizations is to match role demands with styles. Put another way, to ensure that round pegs go in round holes.

Mismanagement Styles

But, personalities like organizations need balance if they are to succeed over time. A good manager may be a strong producer but that manager must at least have an appreciation of other styles if he or she is to be a team player or to succeed over time. In his book, ***How to Solve the MisManagement Crisis,*** Adizes describes classic mismanagers as those who focus exclusively on one role, have limited respect for the importance of other roles and little tolerance for other styles. The four mismanagement styles are characterized as lone rangers, bureaucrats, arsonists, and superfollowers.

Lone Rangers are producers with little or no concern for the other styles. They get to work early and go home late; they're doers that can't delegate significant tasks. Their motto is "Lead, follow, or get the heck out of my way!" After a while the only people left around them are "go-fers," because every once in a while they open their door and yell out, "Go fer this! Go fer that!"

Bureaucrats focus almost exclusively on the administrator role. These people get to work on time and go home on time. They hate mistakes, manage by the book, and seem to prefer being precisely wrong than approximately correct. Unlike lone rangers, they care more about how something was done than the results produced. Their key staff people end up as "yes" people, saying frequently, "Yes, sir" or "Everything's fine, ma'am."

Arsonists are so innovative they never follow through. They would rather create a new idea than work out how to implement an old one. The worst time to work for this kind of entrepreneur is on Monday because they've had all weekend to think and come up with new directions. They want you to go in this direction and that direction—all at the same time. Their motto is "It's too late to agree with me. I've already changed my mind."

Superfollowers focus on playing the integrating role. These are people who've had too much sensitivity training. They are always asking "How do you feel?" They don't want to provide direction because they don't want to offend or push anyone.

They don't get around to doing much, because they're always out trying to get "buy-in."

The Need for Balance

Most people have a dominant style. That is, they are more P than anything else, or more A, E, or I. However, as long as there is a healthy respect for other styles and roles you may have a strong personality, but you don't necessarily have a mismanager. The terms Producer, Administrator, Entrepreneur, and Integrator describe people with some balance and openness to the value of other styles but who are still strong in their focus on, and support of, one key role.

Gerry Faust, author and consultant and former partner of Adizes in his discussion of teamwork, points out that world-class teams are made up of several players with strong and complementary personalities. There is strength in the diversity. There is also conflict. But, the different points of view, the different perspectives provide the opportunity for better, more balanced decisions.

The challenge to an organization comes when it is dominated by one personality or many strong personalities of the same type. An organization of all "Ps" would be hard working, but you should expect a lot of individual effort and little teamwork, considerable focus on today but few thoughts about next year's product line. The long-term goal for organizations is balance of roles and styles.

Yet in the early days of an organization a little imbalance is often a good thing. For example, in its first few months of operation an organization is generally fighting to survive. It needs a strong focus on producing results and a team that has many 'P' style people provides an advantage. In fact, there is little time for A, E, and I activities and too many people with these styles could dangerously distract or slow down the organization.

CORPORATE LIFE CYCLES

In his book of **Corporate Life Cycles,** Adizes talks about the stages organizations go through as they develop. The first stage is **Courtship** where an entrepreneurial thought emerges. During this phase energy and enthusiasm must overcome the naysayers and a strong vision of what could be is needed to pull people out of the comfort of what is. This is a time for the Entrepreneurial role to get extra attention and where the Entrepreneurial style generally dominates. But even at this stage there must be some balance. Some focus on PA and I will be needed to create a successful courtship. If there is only dreaming (E) and no action (P), detailed thought (A) or development of a common sense of mission (I), the dream will go nowhere. The profile of a healthy courtship could be expressed as paEi.

In the next stage, **Infancy,** the organization has been born.

Now it has to be fed. Someone has to produce results, to sell, to do. The "P" role gets more emphasis and more P style people are added to the organization. The profile of the organization shifts to Paei. If the organization succeeds in infancy, if it produces adequate results, the dreaming starts anew. Encouraged by success with one idea and now supported by producers who are implementing the idea, the Entrepreneur tries another, and another, and another. The organization moves quickly into the third stage, **Go-Go.** This stage is characterized by priorities. Too many of them. New ideas are everywhere and everything becomes a priority. People are spread thin. Excitement abounds. Promotions are an hourly event and the Entrepreneurial and Producer styles dominate (PaEi). During this phase people work hard, change is frequent and significant. If an organization stays in this phase too long, people begin to tire. The risk of too many changes too fast begins to build, and service problems can arise. The organization needs to change once again.

The **Adolescent** stage is the answer to the challenges of the Go-Go Stage. It is a time when the organization attempts to get its act together. The drive for more gives way to the time for better. During a healthy adolescence the energy for change moves from new products and services to better products, customer service, teamwork, and planning. The organization attempts to digest the growth it has generated and build its digestive system for new growth. It is a time for pAEi. This is usually a difficult time for the founder because the focus is now on getting organized and establishing systems and the entrepreneurial focus is on building a better organization (First Curve thinking) not creating a new business (Second Curve thinking).

Successfully navigating through this period can be made more difficult by what Adizes calls the "founder trap." This is a trap that the founder falls into when he or she does not learn to delegate or to accept the input of others or is unwilling to give up spur of the moment, intuitive flights of management fancy which send the organization off in new directions without proper planning or preparation.

If, however, the organization can successfully manage the challenges of adolescence, it emerges as a *Prime* organization. At this stage all four roles are in play and the culture reflects a balance of PAE and I.

The keys to prime are integration, teamwork, and a common sense of mission and vision. These forces allow the powerful diversity of different styles to engage in productive conflict. The learning environment improves decisions, communication, effectiveness, and efficiency.

Living in a Two-Curve World

The Prime organization is at the doorstep of world-class status. Now, short-term First Curve thinking (producers and administrators) are complemented by long-term Second Curve thinking (entrepreneurs and integrators). As long as these coexist the organization will maintain its Prime status. When that's done effectively, all four voices are heard—particularly on the Steering Committee. Why is that important? Maybe this scenario will help answer that question.

Suppose you were to divide your managers into groups and give them the same problem to solve. What is the probability that all the groups would come up with the same solution? Zero, because problem solving and decision making are a function of many variables. Is there then any way you could determine which group would come up with the best solution? The answer is, probably! Adizes suggests the probability of a good solution is determined by two factors.

1. Who is in the group
2. How well the group worked together

The first factor will determine whether you have all four styles represented; if any is missing, the solution will be weakened because each style looks at the world in a different way.

For example, if two brothers are fighting over a toy, there are different ways an adult could deal with the situation. A producer would grab the toy and say, "Neither of you get to play with it"— that'll get the job done quickly. An administrator will set up a system: "Jerry, you get to play with the toy from 1 to 3 and Alex from 3 to 5." An entrepreneur will come up with a new and innovative idea: "Let's go to the movies." An integrator will deal with the human interaction issue: "Brothers shouldn't fight. Let's talk."

The second factor determines whether all styles are heard. If you ask "How did you all get along?" and the answer is, "Fine," don't believe it. These styles see the world differently, conflict is inevitable. Faust would argue that world-class teams have all four styles actively involved in the leadership and management. "No one manager can manage alone," Faust writes, "All of us have blind spots. All have strengths and weaknesses. The different styles are complementary and in conflict. The challenge is to make the conflict productive, to create a productive collision of ideas."

Faust has pointed out that all of us have a filter that sits between our senses and our brain which focuses us on different things depending on our styles. Given an identical set of events P's process on some predictable aspects of what they see, A's process on something different. The only way to get the whole picture is to see the same event through four different filters. Like the blind men and the elephant, all styles can feel a different part of the creature. We work together well when we listen to what the other blind men are telling us, and we make better decisions when we fashion solutions based on all of the different perspectives.

The Importance of Climate and Process

While it is essential that the Steering Committee have all four styles represented because of its key balancing role in working with both the F and P design teams, it may be appropriate to divide up the roles when assigning leadership to the two curves and the corresponding P and F Teams. Since producers and administrators are present-time thinkers, they would be best suited for work on a P Team maintaining the First Curve while the Second Curve is being developed. Entrepreneurs and integrators, being long-term thinkers, would function best on an F Team leading the Second Curve efforts.

When there are conflicting needs and demands between present and future, it's the job of the Steering Committee to settle the arguments and maintain the delicate balance between the two sectors. But how can you keep the P and F teams and their design teams from the perils of mismanagement because of expected dominance by only certain styles? According to Faust, good managers, although they may have a dominant style, can under the right conditions look at things from different perspectives. The right conditions include (1) a climate of respect and trust and a strong agreed sense of purpose, and (2) the appropriate amount of structure in the creative, problem-solving, or decision-making process. The climate provides the condition for learning flexible thinking and productive conflict and the structure focuses the attention of participants. It can be used to force consideration of issues as seen through different "style" filters. A method that specifically facilitates responsible problem solving is the Lyles Seven Step method, which follows:

- Define the problem
- Set objectives
- Develop alternative solutions

- Plan implementation
- Troubleshoot the plan
- Communicate the plan
- Implement

The natural tendency for a P is to want to "get on with it." After a few moments of discussion they want to plan the implementation—if they are willing to plan at all. The P style manager will work to ensure the team moves on and gets the decision to the field. The A style manager will want to go into great detail to define the problem. They will want to collect data and work on the details of each step. The E style manager may be bored with the details of problem definition, but will certainly have lots of alternatives. The I style manager will, of course, want to facilitate everyone through the process, will ensure involvement, and will be concerned about getting agreement on each step before the team goes on. They will also have great input when it comes to troubleshooting the plan (e.g., "How will the people in the field feel about this?")

Not every team will have a P, an A, an E, and an I style person, especially in a two-curve world, but every team can strive to create a learning environment and put enough structure in their process to ensure more balanced decisions. In fact, by getting agreement to go through all these steps the good facilitator can get the entire team to take time to define the problem clearly, work to come up with additional creative alternatives, con-

135

sider how others will react, and be sure the team keeps going until it makes a decision and implements it. When that occurs, all four ways of thinking can be heard even though all four styles may not be present. This would be a helpful methodology for the Steering Committee, the P and F Design Teams, and their corresponding P and F Teams.

Exceptional Leaders Needed

It is not easy to maintain Prime and keep all four voices and short-term and long-term thinking alive in the same organization. If you're not careful Mother Nature could begin to exert some pressure. The natural tendency is to relax, to reduce the level of Second Curve thinking because of the short-term advantage of First Curve thinking. The tendency is to say "We used to have to take chances like that." As the ability and willingness to stretch and change decrease, the organization can lose its vitality and begin to age. In other words, it could become a First Curve casualty before the Second Curve has even begun to build.

It takes special leaders on the Steering Committee to protect Second Curve thinking, because as we're suggesting, when push comes to shove, present-time concerns prevail. That's why accounting and finance, sales and marketing, personnel and human resource development, and production and quality often have to be separated in a maturing organization. Left together, the short-term issues of accounting, sales, production, and personnel would dominate. Sales this month become more important than next year's marketing plan, getting the payroll out this month pre-empts the development of a long-term financial plan, etc.

Typically, immediate concerns rule the day. Only when things are moving along reasonably smooth are less immediate concerns able to move to the foreground. Which is natural. You have to win today's battles in order to be eligible to fight again tomorrow. But, having said that does not mean that you should fight today with reckless abandon, without any thought to the battles ahead. Therefore, even in the heat of the immediate fight, you must be preparing for the next. Some resources must be riding out front to assess what lies ahead.

If you send men and supplies ahead when the intensity of the existing battle is such that no one can be spared, you put the commander in an extremely difficult position. He under-stands the logic for sending scouts ahead, yet can't see how he can pull anyone off the front line without setting himself—and his troops—up for defeat.

Today's business leaders see themselves in a similar posi-tion—between a rock and a hard place. The Second Curve must find support, for the First Curve will not last forever. And that support can only come from one source—today's cash flow. Which means that tomorrow's success will depend upon today's sacrifices. And in an age in which all attention seems focused on short-term financial results, sacrifice is a difficult word to absorb. Today's leaders must be willing to invest in something that will some day come to replace all that they worked so hard to achieve. They built the First Curve, and thus see it as an extension of themselves. To divert money away from it, and toward something that will ultimately come to replace it, is understandably difficult to do. Yet, it has to be done. The company's future may be at stake. Therefore, if the current leadership is unable or unwilling to make the necessary sacrifices, they may have to be replaced by those who will.

How will you know whether or not your current leadership is up to the task? Typically, you won't. Or at least not with any degree of certainty. However, there are some things that you can look for which will provide you with at least the basis of an answer.

The best place to begin is to determine the company's position along the First Curve. Remember that, ideally, Second Curve activity should begin at point A on the First Curve before that curve begins to wane. If the company has passed that point and has reached point B or, even worse, point C, the current leadership has probably been discredited for having led the organization downhill. As a result, they may have to be replaced by a new leadership team which brings with it renewed energy and a different mindset.

If, on the other hand, First Curve performance is adequate, and thus, there is no need for turnover within the leadership ranks, a more thorough assessment of their capabilities and characteristics is required. To assist you in this effort, you may find the following questions about your leadership to be of some value:

- Are they willing to change themselves by shedding the role of parent and adopting the role of partner?
- Do they understand that there is a need for both curves to exist simultaneously?
- Are they ready to commit the necessary funds and resources to support the work of both curves?
- Are they willing to demonstrate the type of public support that is necessary to convey strong organizational commitment to both curves?
- Do they have the willingness and ability to articulate the critical importance of the work of one curve to the other, and vice versa?
- Are they willing to remove unyielding obstacles to the new vision, regardless of their power or position?
- Are they able to help others to overcome fear and uncertainty as they seek to create change?
- Are they willing to preserve and protect those who see the vision and want to work for it?
- Are they willing to show how human they are by admitting when they don't know the answer?

Responsibilities of the Steering Committee

Once your top leadership is in place, they should function as the Steering Committee to provide direction and support to both corporate-wide design teams.

Providing for P Design Team Needs

- **Boundaries.** On the one hand, you want the architects of the improved company to be creative and entrepreneurial; on the other hand, you don't want them to squander the family fortune. Somehow an effective balance must be struck between creativity and control. Two of the most powerful mechanisms that can be used for these purposes are the use of belief systems (vision, mission statement, and core values) and performance measures (desired profit margin, return on investment, etc.).

- **Examples.** "Walking the talk" has to be one of the most overused management clichés of all time, yet its frequency of use does little to diminish its importance to the change initiative. The leadership must make every effort to become living symbols of the newly minted corporate culture. And to assist members of the executive team in fulfilling this requirement, sufficient organizational support should be provided. Typically, this support comes in the form of training and the implementation of an effective feedback system. The current favorite is the so-called 360° performance evaluation system, which was popularized by Jack Welch as he sought to transform GE. When asked to describe the system, he responded:

To imbed our values, we give our people 360° evaluations, with input from superiors, peers and subordinates. These are the roughest evaluations you can get, because people hear things about themselves they've never heard before. But they get the input they need, and then the chance to improve.

- **Celebrate Progress.** Catching people doing something right is still the best way to develop people and to create a culture open to ongoing change. It's essential that leaders ensure that short-term wins are systematically planned for, created, and celebrated. If this is done well, people begin to see that the things they thought were impossible not only are possible but are happening and being rewarded.

- **Enlist the Best People.** The company's immediate future is to a large extent in the hands of this group, so its members should be the best the company has to offer. They should be intelligent, energetic, tenacious, and should have a track record of putting the interests of the organization above their own self-interests. Once these highly talented individuals have been identified, they must be pried away from their current endeavors and adequately trained in their new duties.

- **Manage the Politics.** Change team members typically are long on enthusiasm and short on positional power. As a consequence, some of their change-resistant "bosses" can be expected to make attempts at undermining their efforts. They may even resort to using "seagull tactics"—flying in, dumping on somebody, and then flying out whenever the urge moves them. This must not be allowed to happen. Each member of the change team must be made to feel that their support is there when needed.

To ensure this happening, leaders must be prepared to

establish a process for resolving conflicts, and a program for training managers on how to face reality, accept criticism, and engage in open communication. And this will not be easy to do, for in many companies conflict and confrontation is suppressed rather than supported. Leaders in particular don't like to be confronted because they assume that they should be all-knowing and very much in control of things. But control kills invention, learning, and commitment.

Conflict can jump-start the creative process. Emotions often accompany creative tension, and these emotions can be unpleasant. At Intel, for example, conflict is blunt, at times brutal.

"If you're used to tennis," says one observer, "Intel plays rugby, and you walk away with a lot of bruises. They've created a company that takes direct, hard-hitting disagreement as a sign of fitness. You put it all behind you in the locker room, and it's forgotten by the scrimmage the next day."

- **A Sense of Urgency.** Lawrence A. Bossidy, CEO of Allied Signal, says he believes in the "burning platform" theory of change.

When the roustabouts are standing on the offshore oil rig and the foreman yells, "Jump into the water," not only won't they jump but they also won't feel too kindly toward the foreman. There may be sharks in the water. They'll jump only when they themselves see the flames shooting up from the platform.

The leader's job is to help everyone see that the platform is burning, whether the flames are apparent or not.

- **Obstacles Removed.** As the First Curve vision is crafted, and the organization begins to move toward it, hurdles will appear: senior executives who refuse to buy in; an outdated compensation and performance-appraisal system that forces people to choose between the new vision and their own self-interest; inappropriate rules aimed at keeping the boss, rather than the customer happy. These will need to be eliminated or replaced. Typically, only the Steering Committee can do that.

- **Involvement.** Leadership must work hard to guarantee that every employee participates in shaping the transformation process. This is where having every employee on a team pays off.

- **Trust.** If they are to establish a strong foundation of trust, leaders must show employees not only that they mean them no harm but that prospective changes are in everyone's best interest. For this feeling to develop, those in charge must be perceived as having a clear view of where the organization is going, how they plan to get there, and how they are going to include everyone else in the journey. The greatest element in trust-building is, as always, the dissemination of business information to people in all roles and at all levels throughout the organization.

Providing for F Design Team Needs

Many of the needs of the First Curve P Design Team are also those of the Second Curve F Design Team—i.e., examples, trust, involvement, removal of obstacles, and celebration. In addition, Second Curve people need the following.

- **Freedom.** While the First Curve team needs boundaries, this team needs to be released to imagine and create. It needs an environment where blue-sky thinking can thrive.

- **"Unreasonable People."** Members of this design team must be passionate about the company's future and committed to its long-term survival. They must believe beyond doubt that the company's very existence depends on its ability to continuously reinvent itself. These people must fulfill George Bernard Shaw's requirements for "unreasonable men" by never being content, searching constantly for newer and better ways to do everything.

- **Political Risk-Taking.** Second Curve Design Team members must be thick-skinned and willing to stick their necks out. As Machiavelli stated

  It must be remembered that there is nothing more difficult to plan, more doubtful of success, nor more dangerous to manage, than the creation of a new system. For the initiator has enmity of all who would profit by preservation of the old institution and merely lukewarm defenders in those who would gain by the new ones.

- **Time.** Second Curve people are like an R&D department—they can't be put on the same timetables as the First Curve improvement team. Their focus is not on survival, but on the future. As their work involves research—reading, attending conferences, talking to futurists, etc.—this group particularly needs to have its quiet time protected.

Responsibilities of Design Team Members

In addition to their primary responsibility—designing and developing their particular curve—the members of both design teams will have a number of other responsibilities. Some of the most important of these include the following.

- **Developing a Shared Vision.** The first task for design team members is to develop a mutually agreed-upon picture of how their particular curve (first or second) and focus (present or future) should play out. To encourage and utilize everyone's ideas from their corresponding P and F Teams is vital from the start. That's why the team will require facilitation in their own group process as well as training in listening skills and methods of achieving consensus.

- **Supporting One Another.** The rigors of change can become overwhelming at times, especially for those in the driver's seat. For companies undergoing transformation, the tension and strain can become almost palpable at times. If it is to remain effective under such difficult conditions, each design team's level of mutual support is vital.

    The change team for one large petrochemical company decided to begin each of its meetings with 15 minutes of gripes and concerns. As group members, they would acknowledge just how difficult their work was—but only for 15 minutes. Then for the next 15 minutes the meeting became a brag session in which members showcased all their little victories: the efforts they had made that seemed to be paying off, and the problems that they had turned into successes. In this way team members learned how to understand and support each other as emotional crutches and at the same time begin to feel like a winning team. This gave them the extra energy they needed in order to push on.

- **Working with Others.** Once the team has been aligned, the job can begin by setting up two-way communication with the teams who are working on their curve, as well as communicating organization-wide about their progress and thinking. This is when the rule applies: When in doubt, communicate more, not less.

- **Ensuring Congruence of Action.** One of the major complaints of people in organizations undergoing transformation is that the leaders of the change effort don't always seem to "walk the talk." The Design Team members must remain vigilant, watching for inconsistencies that undermine the credibility of the change effort, and then be willing to confront offenders with their observations.

The Duties of P and F Team Members

What are the specific duties of a member of each team? What kind of mental processes are in place? What is it really like to be a member of a P Team or an F Team? Let's imagine the following scenarios.

A Day in the Life of a P-Teamer

Jesse Balkovich is a quality examiner at the QuadCo Pharmaceutical Corporation, an organization that has been following the two-pronged effort described in this book for three years. In terms of his job description, Jesse is exercising a vigilance that will stand him in good stead as a member of his unit P Team, for he is constantly testing and scrutinizing product, in terms of an exhaustive list of quality criteria. Not only must the array of pharmaceutical products under Jesse's care meet high specifications, he is responsible for developing ever more stringent requirements for present and future output. Because of his evident embrace of the value of continuous improvement, when Jesse's P Team first started up his team members looked to him for leadership. Accordingly, portions of the first few Friday afternoon team meetings were devoted to Jesse's sharing the principles of quality improvement with his team. He taught everyone W. Edwards Deming's principle of always reinforcing improvement, no matter how small, and of putting consequences for quality as close to the performance as possible. By the end of this period of informal training, people on Jesse's P Team were starting to take responsibility for their own quality control.

More importantly, they were beginning to apply quality improvement principles to the way they looked at QuadCo Corp. as a whole. The first evidence that Jesse's leadership had helped the team was that members began to show up at their Friday meetings with lists of low-cost ways the company could improve its operations. Jesse's P Team became a band of scouts who, as they went about their paid staff jobs, were continually identifying slack in systems, gaps between employee behavior and the company's dedication to efficiency, and methods in which people at all levels in the company could add value while lowering cost and turnaround time.

Jesse's P Team, like those throughout the company, was cross-functional. The variety of jobs and work environment represented on the team contributed greatly to its ability to scout for ways to improve systems. Within six weeks, Jesse's team had submitted a draft of a detailed plan for a project to ensure zero defects in production of a new decongestant the company was producing. They were invited to present the plan to the companywide P Design Team and two members of the Steering Committee. As they planned their presentation, Jesse's team co-leader Monica suggested they institute the proactive plan she'd seen used by her husband, a textbook salesperson. Monica explained that, whereas the human mind finds it easy to reject a single idea, when presented with three different options, it has trouble saying "No" to all of them. Monica counseled the team to prepare and present three possible plans for improving the decongestant production system. Each plan would have merits, but their preferred zero-defects option would be shown to combine the best points of the others; in addition, it would be the cheapest.

When their preferred plan was adopted, Jesse's team was elated—their first win! Soon they were sobered by their success and of the awareness they'd created for the company's leaders. Back at them came a request that they designate two team members to work as part-time consultants for a period of eight weeks, helping the people on the production line institute the changes they'd prescribed. It was an example of the company's dedication to having the same people who identified an improvement scheme take whatever part they could in putting it in place.

The approval the team gained for its plan set a standard. Within the next six months, Jesse's P Team had been instrumental in beginning its company improvement attack on a variety of different fronts. The variety was really the result of the cross-functional nature of the team. Ellen, from engineering, used the team to propose hiring a consultant to help the company upgrade its wastewater management system to well beyond federal regulation standards. Bruce, from the HR department, led the way in getting the team to propose that the company eliminate the annual rating system that had been used since the company began in favor of a system that tracked performance measures daily, weekly, and monthly. Arthur, a new hire as an in-house computer software developer, asked the team to help him scout and recommend a new integrated workstation designed to widen the span of management control from one-to-fifteen to one-to-forty-five.

All over the company, similar stories were taking place on "local" P Teams. Biweekly Friday afternoon meetings were becoming scenes of celebration, as one by one the teams at QuadCo discovered a multitude of ways to improve present operations and make their organization increasingly efficient and competitive. The Steering Committee instituted a series of contests, giving employees prizes and awards that effectively recognized the extraordinary brain power of employees playing on those teams. Jesse's team soon found itself in friendly competition with a number of winners across the company. The race was on!

A Day in the Life of an F-Teamer

Kelley Jameson had been excited when she found herself on an F Team at Brandon-Weiss Bakeries, a supplier to many major fast-food chains. She had always seen herself as forward-looking, a bit of a dreamer. From the description of what the F Teams would do, Kelley thought it would be right up her alley. The first few team meetings, however, were frustrating for her and for other members. Drawn from across departmental boundaries, the members seemed to be individuals who preferred their own visions and ways of behaving. The company facilitator explained that, before undertaking their actual work, it was important for teams focusing on the future of the company to first come to agreement on their mission, and to set some guidelines for working together. That proved to be easier said than done.

Kelley wasn't sure, to begin with, that she was going to get along with all her new team members. Kelley found Horace, a baker, particularly annoying from the start. She squared off against him in some early discussions, but the disagreement was adroitly handled by the company facilitator. After letting Kelley and Horace go at it for awhile, the facilitator said, "I don't know whether you're aware of it but you two are proving two important things to the team—A, that disagreements are inevitable, and B, that you're both tremendously creative people. In short, the team needs both of you critically. Though it may be difficult at first, I want both of you to be watching for instances where you *agree,* and communicate agreement to each other."

The truth was that, like Kelley, all members of the team were individuals. They were by nature imaginative and intuitive, and tended to trust far more in their versions of the world than they did in generally accepted notions they saw around them. Consequently, it was going to take longer for these don't-go-along-with-the-crowd people to become a "crowd." For instance, it took fully three meetings before the team agreed that they needed to follow these guidelines:

- Trust an intuitive hunch first, then give it at least three checks before submitting it to the team.
- It's okay and healthy to disagree. Just make sure your disagreement is around ideas, not personalities.
- Participate fully in structured exercises designed to teamwork around imagination and creativity.

This last agreement proved to be a critical one for the team's development as a team. Members participated in a series of creativity/team-building activities facilitated by consultants from Synergic Consultants, whose model of blending traditional team-development theories with free-wheeling creativity constructs had been proven useful by organizations like Brandon-Weiss. Kelley especially relished one exercise where the team was working on solving a problem related to the elasticity of bagel dough. They were acting out the recipe and Horace was supposed to be the leavening. Kelley had fun pretending to "add water" to Horace's ingredient by tossing shredded paper over him. Instead of showing irritation, Horace played his part, sighing with pleasure. He was such a good sport that Kelley decided she wanted him for a friend.

The Kelley-Horace combination soon proved themselves a dynamic duo. They went to work on an in-depth study of where fast-food fads would be by the year 2001. Using the recent start-up of gourmet bagel businesses as a model, they came up with a way of projecting upscale tastes in America that took into account international influences. Presenting their plan to the F Team, they found that members were wowed by the simplicity and order of their projection model. Everyone wanted to help prepare it for submission to the companywide F Design Team. George, from customer service, who had a background in drama, said "I want to work up a way to dramatize this for selling it to the Steering Committee." At the next meeting, George handed out scripts and started rehearsing the members in a short but dynamic skit. Meanwhile, two other members, who had artistic and computer skills, had showed up with storyboards for a multimedia show on the subject. When Kelley and Horace saw the enthusiasm their work had generated on the team, they gave each other high-fives.

We hope these scenarios give you a flavor of the potential of P and F Teams. While they will cost your company time and money, the investment should prove well worth it.

Final Thoughts

The final key to creating world-class status involves helping people with differing viewpoints to partner together. Since you are trying to live in a two-curve world, seeing differences as assets instead of problems is essential. While sometimes it's best to separate the two ways of thinking, the most elegant ideas come out of a grand mix. This mix is particularly important on the Steering Committee that sits at the bridge of the spaceship and balances the need to maintain the ship in good operating condition, while planning its journey into the future.

CHAPTER FIVE

DO I HAVE WHAT IT TAKES TO LIVE IN A TWO-CURVE WORLD?

"Our deepest fear is not that we are inadequate. Our deepest fear is that we are powerful beyond measure. It is our light, not our darkness, that most frightens us. We ask ourselves, who am I to be brilliant, gorgeous, talented, and fabulous? Actually, who are you not to be? You are a child of God. Your playing small doesn't serve the world. There is nothing enlightened about shrinking so that other people won't feel insecure around you. We are born to make manifest the Glory of God that is within us. It's not just in some of us, it's in everyone, and as we let our own light shine, we consciously give other people permission to do the same. As we are liberated from our own fear, our presence automatically liberates others."

—Nelson Mandela, Inaugural address.

In many ways, what we have done to you in this book is similar to what a young minister did to an old farmer. Asked to be a guest preacher at a rural church, the young minister headed up the highway from his home in the city. On the way he got caught in a snow storm. Luckily he had started out early enough that he still got to the church on time even though twelve inches of snow had fallen. When he entered the church there was only one person in attendance, an old farmer. The minister waited for awhile to see if anyone else was coming. When no one did, he approached the old farmer and said: "You're the only one here. What do you think I should do?"

The farmer smiled and said "I'm just an old farmer and don't know a great deal. But there's one thing I do know! If only one horse came to the barn, I'd feed him."

"That's fair enough," replied the young minister. So he headed to the pulpit and began the service. When he got to the sermon, the young minister got carried away. He ranted and raved. When he finally gave the benediction he looked at his watch and an hour and a half had gone by since he started the service. He jumped down from the pulpit and stood in front of the old farmer once again. "Well! What did you think?" the young minister asked.

The old farmer thought for a minute and then said, "I'm just an old farmer and don't know a great deal. But there's once thing I do know! If only one horse came to the barn I wouldn't give him **the whole load!**"

Our fear with this book is that we might have given you the whole load and overwhelmed you, not only with information but the magnitude of the task before you. As one small business owner told us:

> As the leader of a small business, what you're proposing—managing the present and creating the future at the same time—seems almost overwhelming. I think "Wow. Great ideas!" We're even doing some of them. But it would take all of my organization's time to put what you're talking about into practice, even with 30 employees and that would leave little time for business. It makes me ask: Is our business remote data acquisition and reporting or building a world-class organization?

STAGES OF CONCERN

ur answer would be "both." But we have to listen to the concern. In fact, research originally conducted by Gene Hall and his colleagues at the University of

Texas suggests that people who are faced with change express six predictable and sequential concerns. As you read about these concerns, be aware of which ones you, the reader, may have been experiencing as you have encountered the ideas in this book.

1. **Information Concerns.** What is a two-curve world all about? Why is it needed? What is wrong with the way things are now?

    When you have information concerns you don't want to be sold on the change; you simply want to understand it. Our goal in writing this book has been to provide you with the kind of information that allows you to reach your own conclusions about the value of such an organization. (We apologize if we over-sold and under-informed, but you probably have moved beyond this first concern and are more focused on the next few concerns.)

2. **Personal Concerns.** How will living in a two-curve world impact me personally? What's in it for me? Will I win or lose? How will I find the time? Do I have the skills and resources to implement the necessary changes in my area?

    These personal concerns have to be addressed in such a way that you feel you have been heard. It has been said that **"What you resist, persists."** If you don't permit people to deal with their feelings about what's happening, these feelings stay around. The corollary to this principle is that *if you deal with what is bothering you, in the very process of dealing with your feelings, the concerns often go away.*

Have you ever said to yourself, "I'm glad I got that off my chest?" If so, you know the relief that comes from sharing your feelings with someone. Just having a chance to talk about your concerns during change clears your mind and stimulates creativity that can be used to help rather than hinder change efforts. This is where listening comes in. Leaders and managers must permit people to express their personal concerns without living in fear of evaluation, judgment, or retribution.

Personal concerns are the most overlooked and undermanaged concerns in the change process. If you don't take the time to address individual needs and fears, you won't get people beyond this basic level of concern. For that reason, let's look at some of the key personal concerns people often have with regard to change. See if any of these are concerns you have right now about what we are suggesting in this book.

- ***People get concerned about the awkward, ill-at-ease, and self-conscious feelings they have.*** Change means doing something different, so people will always feel this way. (In fact, if you don't feel awkward during a period of change, you're probably not doing anything different.) Living in a two-curve world should create some awkwardness because everyone will have to think and act differently than they have in the past. When you see it in yourself or some of your people don't think there is something wrong—recognize it as a natural occurrence.

159

- ***People initially focus on what they have to give up.*** Change is a very individual matter. It throws people. The bottom drops out. The security blanket is gone. It's only human nature: people's first reaction to a suggested change tends to be a personal sense of loss. The effective leader understands that when people go through change they have a need to mourn their losses. What do we mean by "losses"? These include, among other things, the loss of control, of time, of order, of resources, of co-workers, of prestige. In order to help them move forward, leaders need to help people deal with this sense of loss. It may seem silly, but people need to be given a chance to mourn their feelings of loss, perhaps just by having time to talk with others about how they feel. Remember, what you resist persists. Getting in touch with what you think you will be losing in a two-curve world will help you accept some of the benefits.

- ***People feel alone even if everyone else is going through the same change.*** When change hits, even if everyone around us is facing the same situation most of us tend to take it personally "Why me?" The irony is that in order for the change to be successful, we need the support of others. In fact, we need to *ask* for such support. People are apt to feel punished when they have to learn new ways of working. If change is to be successful, people need to recruit the help of those around them. We need each other. This is why support groups work when people are facing changes or times of stress in their lives. They need to feel that their leaders (partners), co-workers, and families are on their side in terms of supporting the changes they need to make. Remember, you can't create a world-class organization by yourself. You need the support of others, and they need your support.

- ***People can handle only so much change.*** Beyond a few changes—or even only one, if the change is significant—people tend to get overwhelmed and become immobilized. That's why we suggested not changing everything all at once. Pick out the key areas that will make the biggest difference. Maybe start by setting up the P and F Team process. Whatever you do, make sure people have some success experiences to build on before implementing more changes.

- ***People are at different levels of readiness for change.*** Although almost everyone experiences some resistance to change, some individuals may quickly get excited by an opportunity to implement new ideas; others need some time to warm up to new challenges. This doesn't mean there's any one "right" place to be on the readiness continuum; it just means that people have different outlooks and degrees of flexibility toward what they've been asked to do. Awareness of one's own level of readiness for change can be extremely helpful in getting one through any change effort. Where are you?

- ***People are concerned that they won't have sufficient resources.*** When people are asked to do more, they often think they need additional time, money, facilities, and personnel. But the reality today is that they will have to do more with less. In organizations that have downsized there are fewer people around, and those that are around are being asked to accept new responsibilities; they need to work smarter rather than harder. Rather than providing these resources directly, leaders must help people to discover their own ability to generate them. The Steering Committee and the P and F Design Teams could be helpful here, keeping people focused while fostering two-way communication. It would be particularly helpful if they could:

- provide consistent messages about vision and goals
- remind people that the change is important
- provide forums for people to speak their minds
- offer encouragement and reassurance
- provide resources that help resolve concerns—time, money, management support, clear expectations

Once people feel that their personal concerns have been addressed, they tend to turn their attention to how the change will be implemented. We bet you have many questions in this concern area.

3. ***Implementation Concerns.*** What do I do first? second? third? How do I manage all the details? What happens if it doesn't work as planned? Where do I go for help? How long will this take? Is what I am experiencing typical?

People with implementation concerns are focused on the details involved in making the change a reality. In the past, the expectation was that top management would answer all these questions. However, our "everyone a change agent" philosophy tells us that these questions can be answered only through the involvement of all who are impacted by the change.

We probably shared enough information about the P and F Team process and the organizationwide Design Teams and Steering Committee structure to stimulate your interest, but not enough for you to feel confident about setting all this up in your organization tomorrow. You may wonder why we didn't give more specific examples of this process and structure in practice. The reality is that while many organizational leaders realize they have to manage the present and create the future at the same time, few of them have taken the time to do it. Remember, this book was intended to be thought-provoking and motivating, not a how-to manual. The P and F Team process is intriguing to us. While we have seen bits and pieces of it, it does not presently exist in totality. The nearest to it is the work that Gelinas James Akiyoshi have been doing with organizations like Levi-Strauss & Co., Chevron Research and Technology, Pacific Gas & Electric, the medical center at Vanderbilt University, and Blanchard Training and Development, Inc. In fact, we want to do some research on world-class organizations and follow this publication with a field book that contains the best thinking about and delivery of the key ideas presented here. If you know of any two-curve success stories or are doing some exciting things yourself, please let us know.

Where does this leave you? To ponder the ideas we have shared and design your own unique path to world-class leadership. The reality is, you have no choice but to manage the present and create the future at the same time. After all, they are bumping into each other every day.

If you accept the assignment and believe it is **mission possible,** you and other leaders in your organization can assure a successful journey by:

- aligning systems (performance planning, tracking, feedback, and evaluation systems) with your world-class journey
- offering perspective about how long things should take and whether performance is on-track
- providing training and coaching on how to implement the necessary changes
- looking for small wins, recognizing progress
- sharing excitement and optimism about the world-class journey

Once people have resolved their implementation concerns, they are more likely to be open and ready to evaluate on its merits the impact of the change.

4. **Impact Concerns.** Is the effort worth it? Is the change making a difference?

People with impact concerns are interested in whether the change is paying off. This is the stage where people sell themselves on the benefits of the change. It's interesting to note that in the past this was always the first (and many times the only) concern that change agents addressed in implementing change. Selling benefits seemed to be what making change was all about. Now we know that impact is only the fourth concern people have in the change process; unless and until their information, personal, and implementation concerns have been addressed, the benefits of the change will be perceived as mere empty promises.

This is why we have tried not to oversell our ideas. We have risked our credibility with you by admitting that we don't have everything all thought out. When we were writing this book we did not want to act like "know-it-alls." Instead, together we hope we can make progress by:

- Collecting and sharing information and success stories.
- Creating rituals and events that anchor movement toward world-class status.
- Working with people to restructure organizations in ways that support a two-curve world.
- Removing obstacles to implementation.
- Facilitating problem solving along the way.

After people hear about the benefits of change, they're ready to consider involving other people in the process. This might take awhile.

5. ***Collaboration Concerns.*** Who else should be involved? How can we work with others to get them involved in what we are doing? How do we spread the word?

People with collaboration concerns are focused on cooperating with others to get the job done. They want to get everyone on-board because they're convinced that the change is making a difference. This is the level of the true believer, that person who has experienced the change and believes that the benefits of the change exceed the efforts and problems encountered in making it happen. Such people become committed to fully implementing the change by spreading the word about its benefits and helping others to implement. This is our hope and dream—spreading the word and involving as many people as possible in world-class journeys. Will you join us on that quest? This involves encouraging teamwork and interdependence and cheerleading people on the journey.

After collaboration concerns come concerns about improving and refining the original change initiative.

6. ***Refinement Concerns.*** How can we make the change even better? Can we improve on our original idea?

People with refinement concerns are moving from focusing on implementation to recreating the future. They have a world-class status mentality. They are ready to design their own destiny, whether that means further improving whatever they are doing now or pushing the boundaries toward more innovative, future-oriented thinking. At this level people are looking beyond the intended change at new and related ways to innovate. What's going on at this stage is a toggling back and forth between present-time implementation and future-time innovation. Sound familiar? This is where we need to go. All aboard! The trip involves supporting continuous improvement and innovation as well as encouraging others to challenge the status quo.

A CONTINUOUS IMPROVED CULTURE

In the Delivery stage of any change, whether the change is generated from a P Team or F Team, people will have these concerns. If they successfully pass through them, they will be ready to help plan the next change, almost before the first one is completely in place. This openness to ongoing change is critical to living in a two-curve world where the present and the future are meeting on a day-to-day basis. The role of the leader is crucial here, because with each successive pass through these stages, organizations develop their capacity to move through change more effectively.

We envision that the organization of the future will have everyone helping each other live and work effectively in a state where things are always somewhat disconcertingly out of place. As everyone is involved in change efforts through their work with one of the two design teams, so everyone must be involved in implementing the plans that emerge from these efforts. We think the assumption of the future is that everyone has power (i.e., the capacity to channel energy and make things happen), and that it's the job of leaders to facilitate the creation of organizational structures that release this power.

This involves bringing out the best in people. In presenting to business audiences we often ask, "Given the fact that you have to spend 8, 10, or 12 hours a day at work, would you rather be ordinary or magnificent?" Nobody ever seems to choose ordinary. Given a chance, people would like to be magnificent. And yet, what kind of behavior dominates in organizations? Ordinary! Why?

Somehow we've all grown up expecting the ordinary. We've come to think of magnificence as being in short supply, and we treat people accordingly. Not surprisingly, they respond in kind—low expectations lead to low performance. Since expecting less becomes a self-fulfilling prophecy, the way to reverse performance begins with reversing expectations.

The Key to Releasing Magnificence

What does it take to trigger magnificence in people? This might not seem an appropriate thought to put in a management book, but we think that the answer is *unconditional love.* When we talk about unconditional love, we're not saying that people are perfect and without faults, or that they don't make mistakes. We just support the philosophy expressed in **The One Minute Manager:** "People are okay, it's just their behavior that's a problem sometimes." It's our belief that all people are sources of magnificence, but that certain things block the expression of their greatness.

Whenever we present this idea, we imagine certain people saying to themselves, "Yeah, right. You don't know about Henry!" We will be the first to acknowledge the existence of "Henrys" in most of our lives. On the other hand, this bringing to mind of Henry's worst aspects is illustrative of one of the major influences that block people's expression of their magnificence. It is what we might call the Henry-in-the-eye-of-the-beholder. It is our **expectations of Henry to mess up**. One of the most powerful rules we have discovered in the field of management science is that...

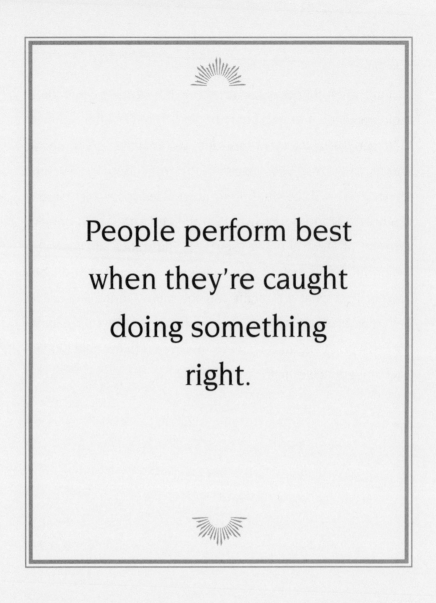

People perform best
when they're caught
doing something
right.

By and large, people will deliver on your expectations. If you expect them to perform well, and demonstrate that expectation in your interactions with them (including both praisings and reprimands), they will begin to show you signs of the good of which they're capable. Keep it up, and pretty soon they'll reveal their magnificence. Our guess about most of the "Henrys" of the world is that, while they've had plenty of people catching them doing things wrong, they've not had anyone catching them doing things right lately.

The Human Ego

If catching people doing things right is such a powerful strategy, why do so many leaders and managers stay focused on catching people doing things wrong? It's a self-esteem problem. Walt Kelley's cartoon possum Pogo was right when he said, "We have met the enemy, and he is us." This is where the negative self-fulfilling prophecy begins. If you don't feel good about yourself, you can't help other people in your organization to feel good about themselves. If those others don't feel good about themselves, they can't release their magnificence through outstanding work. So bringing out the best in others begins with accepting your own magnificence.

The biggest addiction in the world today is not to drugs or alcohol. It is to the human ego. When you are ego driven you take yourself too seriously. There are two types of ego-centeredness: ***self-doubt*** and ***false pride***. Both are enemies of magnifi-

171

cence. People with self-doubt are consumed with their own shortcomings and tend to be hard on themselves. People with false pride have a distorted image of their own importance and see themselves as the center of the universe.

It's easy to understand that self-doubt comes from lack of self-esteem, because people afflicted with it on a daily basis act as if they are worth less than others. These people need to remind themselves, "Rich or poor, smart or dumb, beautiful or ugly, naughty or good—I am a valuable human being." The cure is less obvious with people suffering from false pride, because even though they behave as if they are the only ones who count, underneath they're really trying to make up for their own lack of self-esteem. Most of them try to compensate for their feeling of being inferior by trying to control things and people around them—especially when they don't know what they're doing. They have a great need to be right, even when it's clear to everyone else that they're wrong. Many of these people, who really feel small inside, figure that the way to be tall is to go around cutting the heads off of others. People suffering from either kind of ego addiction generally have trouble catching others doing things right. The ones with self-doubt still can't trust their own judgment enough to praise someone else's work—while the ones with inflated opinions of themselves hesitate to build others up because they think that doing so will take something away from them.

If any of this sounds a bit too close for comfort, don't be alarmed: Even the best of us have traces of self-doubt and false pride. All of us get in our own way at times as a result of the machinations of the "enemy" that Pogo identified. Someone once told us that EGO stands for **E**dging **G**od **O**ut. When our ego is allowed to eat our brain, our thinking blurs and we lose the sense of our connection with a spiritual home base, with others, and with our true, magnificent selves. In this state, it seems to us that we must achieve in order to earn our magnificence, rather than let achievement flow directly from our magnificence. When this kind of delusion sets in, the trick is to try to remember who we really are because all of us are actually cases of mistaken identity.

Spiritual Amnesia

Every human being might be said to be suffering from a kind of spiritual amnesia. For most of us, the sense of mystery concerning where we came from and where we are going, which we knew and felt as little children, has been replaced in the process of "growing up" by a veneer of reasonableness and false certainty. Focused as we are on our day-to-day routines, we are sleepwalkers in the land of little. Moving about in a dream of assumed constraints, it is difficult or impossible for us to imagine just how great we could be. We are waiting for someone to come along and recognize the Selves we have forgotten. A simple story illustrates this well.

In a palace there once lived a prince (or, if you like, a princess). One day, just for fun, the prince disguised himself as a commoner and went into town. No one recognized him, so he decided to visit places where princes never go. As he was going down a dark street, he was attacked by two robbers. In the scuffle he received a sharp blow on the head. He was left in a heap, unconscious and alone. When he came to, the prince had completely forgotten who he was.

He floated about for days in a sort of dream, sleeping in alleyways and begging for scraps, and before long he'd become a tramp. Something always seemed to be calling to him, but he could not recall who he was or where he lived, and there was nobody around to recognize him for who he really was. One night some of his courtiers found him asleep in a park. They carried him home to the palace, cleaned him up, and put him to bed. The next morning the prince awoke and knew his bedroom as if for the first time. After a short period, during which he was treated as if he were wise and worthy of the utmost respect, the prince recollected his true identity. He came to regard his adventure in the village as only a dream.

To us, this story is really about the nobility and magnificence just waiting to be reawakened in every person. It clearly isn't enough for leaders to work on their organizations—they must go to work on themselves. When your outlook is driven by your ego, your life is dominated by fear. It's hard for you to see past what got you to where you are today, so you tend to defend it and resist challenges to the status quo. But in today's hotly competitive markets, steering your car by the rear-view mirror is a recipe for disaster. History offers some compelling illustrations of how even the best of us can misinterpret clues about the future when we use yesterday's logic.

- A 1910 edition of **Scientific American** proclaimed that "to affirm that the aeroplane is going to 'revolutionize' naval warfare of the future is to be guilty of the wildest exaggeration."
- On November 16, 1929, The Harvard Economic Society agreed that "a severe depression like that of 1920–1921 is outside the range of possibility."
- After concluding the nonaggression pact with Hitler in 1939, Stalin was so convinced the Germans would not attack that he ignored 84 warnings to the contrary.
- In 1943 Thomas J. Watson, then chairman of IBM, was quoted as saying that he believed there to be "a world market for about five computers."
- In 1977, Ken Olson, then president of DEC, stated that "there is no reason for any individual to have a computer in their home."
- In 1991, a senior executive from CBS told a congressional committee that digital television "defies the laws of physics."

These examples show that being certain is not necessarily a virtue. In fact it's best to admit that you don't know everything, and you might even need help. Living in a two-curve world isn't easy, so the H.E.L.P. acronym on the next page may provide you with a bit of just that.

H stands for Humor.

Most people undergoing change act as if they have
tight underwear on. We need to take seriously
what we do to help people through change—
but take ourselves lightly. The journey need not be grim.
Rule H is: *Lighten up.*

E stands for Esteem.

Conditional esteem depends on favorable conditions
and events. Unconditional esteem comes from realizing
that no matter what happens, your life is meaningful and valuable.
When things go wrong, repeat **Rule E:**
I'm O.K.   I don't need to prove myself.

L stands for Listen.

If we were meant to speak more than listen,
we'd have two mouths. In times of change, sensitivity to
people's concerns is critical. Sometimes they just need to
get things off their chests before they can pick up and go on.
So the **L Rule is:** *Listen more.   Speak less.*

P stands for Praise.

Especially at the beginning of change efforts, when early
successes are critical, people need to catch each other
doing things right. This may mean approximately right,
rather than perfectly right. **Rule P:**
Up the support.   Down the criticism.

HUMOR

Henry Ward Beecher, the noted American clergyman, editor, and writer of the last century, declared: "In things pertaining to enthusiasm, no man is sane who does not know how to be insane on proper occasions." That's probably truer amidst today's turbulence, where the tendency toward grimness and seriousness can blight an organization's environment and limit its creative thinking.

You can tell right away when you visit a company where no one's having any fun—there's no soul in the place. People are longing to lighten up, but they have no permission. G. K. Chesterton knew of the link between humor and the spirit of work when he wrote, "Joking is undignified; that is why it is so good for the soul." So far as we know, the 1990s are the first decade in which leaders and managers are being offered courses in humor. These classes don't teach the art of telling a good joke; they're aimed at helping people contact something they already have inside—their sense of humor. Increasing people's natural ability to see the funny or absurd side of a situation will have a direct bearing on their effectiveness with others. If some of today's leaders don't relearn the value of a smile, they'll be unable to fire up others' ability to find real enjoyment in their work.

So, if your face seems perpetually set in a frown or grimace, start thinking smiles. Become a smile millionaire and people will be glad to see you coming. Besides, it will keep your face youthful. As Mark Twain opined, "Wrinkles should merely indicate where smiles have been."

Humility and Humor

Humility and humor go hand in hand. An attitude of humility is an ingredient of successful change because it permits people to take what they do seriously, while at the same time taking themselves lightly. People with humility don't think less of themselves—they just think about themselves less. Because they're willing to admit their own limitations, they tend to be willing team players.

In the past, managers were reluctant to share their vulnerability with their people. This was seen as weakness, as in the story of the two generals who were talking as they stood on a hill overlooking their troops before going into battle. One general said to his aide, "Bring me my red cape." Confused, the other officer said, "But general, if you wear your red cape, you'll be a clear target for the enemy." The valiant officer replied, "I'm not worried about the enemy, I'm worried about my men. If by chance I am wounded, the blood will blend in with my cape. Unaware that I am hurt, my men will continue to advance. I never want my men to know I am wounded!" With that, the other general turned to his aide and said, "Bring me my brown pants!" These leaders could not bear to appear vulnerable in the presence of their people.

As you work on yourself to develop the human traits that will serve the new strategic order, you will be required to unlearn many of the traits you thought came with the territory of leader. Many leaders today seem to be cursed with a know-it-all attitude. They take themselves too seriously. Confidence—a great asset when it comes to managing the complexities of these times—should never be confused with omniscience. Things are just too complicated for any one person to stay on top of everything. Your journey into the future must begin with a willingness to accept the fact that regardless of how successful you've been in the past there is much out there that you need to know, yet don't know.

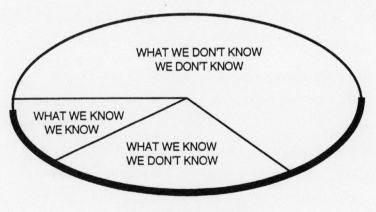

THE KNOWLEDGE PIE

There is a tremendously practical bottom-line outcome when you share your own humanness and vulnerability with people. You build the trust and confidence of others (and thus become approachable), and you contribute to their own receptivity to the mind power of the organization. Once you are freed up to listen to and utilize the synergistic knowledge of those around you, you are utilizing the most powerful secret of the new leadership.

Becoming Childlike

It may seem paradoxical, but as all of us embark on our journey into the complex and uncertain future, the attitude we most need to develop is child-likeness. We must learn to temporarily suspend the inhibitions we have acquired growing up and revisit our playful child. As a friend reminded us when he saw the knowledge pie depicted on page 179, there's an important fourth slice called *what we don't know we know*. Since the tendency amidst change is to forget the most important stuff we've learned, we include the following questions as reminders.

- *Are you willing to be different?* For many, the primary mission in life is conformity; they'll do anything to avoid being out of step. In an organization, this desire for acceptance surfaces most obviously in meetings. Rather than trying to introduce fresh points of view, people go with the flow. Collaboration is important in good problem solving, but if we overemphasize consensus building we may not share enough new facts and points of view.

- ***Does looking good come first?*** If you're overly concerned about what others think of you, you'll misuse a valuable part of your energy by avoiding making mistakes and looking bad in front of others.

- ***Is wasting time a threat to you?*** If you feel the need to account for your actions every waking moment of the day, you won't spend much time visualizing the future or playing with ideas that hold no immediate payoff because you might consider it a waste of time and yet most of history's truly innovative ideas have come from people who made a habit of dreaming.

- ***Are you strictly the nuts-and-bolts type?*** If you want to be seen at all costs as practical, economical, cost-cutting and bottom-line efficient, you may tend to exercise judgment too quickly, rejecting out of hand ideas that are less than complete or perfect, rather than building on them.

- ***How comfortable are you with rocking the boat?*** People who have been taught to be polite and accept things without question don't know how to ask "Why?" without placing others on the defensive. If you worry about expressing doubt or ignorance, being too inquisitive, or asking why about things that everyone accepts, your ability to foretell the future will be impaired.

- ***Can you let others take credit?*** Those who are threatened by admitting that another's idea is better than their own will reject attempts to improve or build on their ideas, thus shutting down much of the brain power available to the group. Remember this thought: You'll be amazed at how much you can get done when you don't worry about who gets the credit.

- *How adventurous are you?* People who desire the safety of the known and familiar tend to strictly define the limits of their comfort zones. New things put them off. Their discomfort prevents them from exploring potential solutions.

- *Are you all for quick solutions?* A killer of innovation is the belief that there is only one right answer to any problem. If you are easily content after finding one workable solution, you are probably missing out on a chance to come up with a better one.

- *How's your trust level?* Do you mistrust others, thinking they'll somehow use your suggestions against you or take credit for your ideas? By holding back on trust, you stifle your own creativity and ultimately limit the growth of your company.

- *Can you give up control?* Some people's biggest fear is being unable to keep everything in place. Leading change is like riding a bucking bronco: sometimes you're in control, but mostly you're not. There's wisdom in striking a balance between making things happen and letting things happen.

- *Can you handle disagreement and criticism?* Unless you're willing and able to meet opposition—and sometimes not to be liked—change will be tough on you. If you are looking for applause all the time, leading a world-class journey might be a long trip.

- *Can you go the distance?* Perhaps you have a short fuse when you've been working overlong on a problem. Once you assume that a goal can't be achieved or a problem solved, you shut down your own creativity and the creativity of those around you.

When you were a child you could have answered "yes" to most of those questions. Can you relearn those things?

ESTEEM

All of the previous questions really relate to self-esteem. While we have already talked about self-esteem, let's see if we can take our thinking a few steps further.

In creating organizations where people can be magnificent, work must go on constantly at the personal as well as the inter-personal level. You can't expect leaders to show unconditional love toward their people when they don't show it toward them-selves. People who have big egos are really second-guessing themselves all the time. They think that one more sale, one more victory, one more status symbol, one more demonstration of power and control, will prove they're okay. But it's like sending a trickle into an empty vat unless they realize they're **already okay**.

In his book ***Ordering Your Private World***, Gordon MacDonald explains the difference between people who are "driven" and those who are "called." Driven people think they own everything—their relationships, possessions, ideas. They spend all their time trying to defend what they own. Called people, on the other hand, think everything is on loan. They don't own anything. Their job is to appreciate and nurture what comes into their lives.

What's different about called people? Why are they less threatened by change? Their secret is that their self-esteem doesn't depend on external events.

Jennifer James equates true self-esteem with safety. When leaders have true self-esteem, they are safe from the fears and worries that plague others and limit their creativity and energy. We call this kind of safety *unconditional self-esteem*.

It can be illustrated by invoking a scene that most of us can remember. Did you ever have the experience as a child of going on a long auto trip with your parents? Recall the feeling, just before drifting off to sleep in the back seat: the hum of the tires...the conversation of your parents drifting from the front seat. With your parents in charge in the front, you had a feeling of tranquillity and utter safety. This is the kind of feeling it's still possible for you to have, even amid all the disruption of fundamental organizational change.

Self-esteem is a choice. Some will say that's simplistic—it doesn't take into account all the mistakes, the failures, the childhood deprivations and put-downs people have experienced that prevent them from realizing they're okay. We know about all that. But we agree with Norman Vincent Peale when he said that every day when you get up, you have a choice to feel good about yourself or to feel lousy about yourself. Norman could never understand why so many good people chose the latter. Neither can we.

LISTEN

When we truly listen to others, it not only brings out the magnificence in them, it does the same for us. One reason we have trouble staying on course and accepting our own magnificence is that we don't take time to quiet ourselves and listen to the reassuring voice that says we are okay. To pray is to let that voice speak to the center of your being and to let it resonate throughout your whole being.

Why is solitude so hard for most of us to bear? Because we are undisciplined as inner listeners. We all have two selves: an inner self that is thoughtful, reflective, and a good listener, and an outer, task-oriented self that is focused on doing and achieving and getting things done. Often we are too busy with our outer self to awaken our inner self.

Like any other relationship, one's relationship with self, the inner self, must be cultivated. Some may ask why this is so, since one's self is so close, so intimate. But this is the very reason the relationship must be kept up: familiarity breeds contempt. Consider the closest relationship many people experience, the one with a spouse. If, through the daily routines that we fall into in waging the battle of life, familiarity is allowed to creep into this relationship, soon the very words or touches of the one lying next to you come to seem merely "more of the same." One day leads to another, life becomes little more than a blur. As Lily Tomlin used to say, "The trouble with being in a rat race is that, even if you win the race, you're still a rat."

To avoid the rat race and stay on course, we must honor the inner self. How is this done? There is only one way: by seeking solitude. We need times when we can be alone with the voice that says, "You are a valuable person." How can you find time for solitude? We recommend that you enter into each day more slowly and deliberately, with a combination of noncompetitive activities that are intrinsically valuable. Such activities might include prayer, meditation, yoga, reflective reading, and a certain kind of exercise. Walking, running, swimming, or biking would be perfect, but you must take care when including exercise in this routine for entering your day, for it is certainly possible to turn it into just another form of competition, even if only with yourself.

William Glasser, who wrote **Positive Addiction**, studied those people he described as having a quality of strength—the ability to meet and deal effectively with the stresses of living. He found that people with this quality took care of themselves; that is, each of them had some routine he or she engaged in (such as running or meditating) that was solitary and noncompetitive, that challenged them and gave them back to themselves. Jim Ballard, a writer who has worked closely with us throughout the development of this book, has been a morning runner for over twenty years. It's fun to be around Jim when someone asks him how far he runs every day. His reply is always, "I don't know." The inquirer, nonplussed, usually counters with, "Well, how long do you run?" Again, Jim will say, "I don't know. My running is just the way I enter my day. It isn't about getting someplace—it's about being someplace."

What a great approach to exercise, and what a great way to start the day: just being in the moment. Steve Covey, author of **The Seven Habits of Highly Effective People**, contends that we need what he calls a "personal victory" each and every day, and that the earlier in the day you can get it, the more the rest of the day will be like icing on the cake.

Of course, no one else is going to see to it that you get the strength building you need to be world-class, and that is as it should be. It is your job to provide for yourself in this way.

You must value yourself enough to undergo the discipline associated with building inner resources. There's bad news and there's good news. The bad news is that every day still has just twenty-four hours in it, and you must make the time for this solitary, thankless activity even if it means (as it often does) getting up earlier each morning than you presently do. The good news is that on the other side of your routine—the coming home from the long, dark run or walk, the completion of the quiet sitting or reflective reading or journal writing—you savor an earned joy, a pure sense of self that the world can never give.

The Need for Quiet Time

Throughout this book we have emphasized that organizations are in constant "whitewater," with one change unfolding on top of another, and little time to solidify or refine order. If a company is to be proactive about the future amid this state of perpetual chaos, both organizational and individual discipline will be required to carve out thinking and planning time.

Any metaphor for change can be misleading, and the whitewater image is no exception. The picture of modern change as a turbulently flowing river gives the impression that things must constantly be in turmoil. Actually, each whitewater section of a river is preceded and followed by a calmer flow. Every peak is followed by a valley. The "secret sauce" of our book is to suggest that everyone in the organization must be encouraged to use some of his/her discretionary time to either improve or refine present operations or to scan the horizon for tidal waves that may soon be breaking on the beach.

All of the significant advances in human history, great social and political reformations, artistic productions, unique inventions, etc., have come not from the day-to-day rushing around, the meaningless activity, but rather from periods of deep and rigorous contemplation. In the same way, before a great organization's future can unfold, there must be reflective thinking.

The forward-looking organization therefore must provide its people with the opportunity to slow things down to plan and prepare. This means that its leaders must break the habit of busy-as-usual. The puritan work ethic may be about to meet its match: true organizational efficiency.

In most companies today, it's as if we all had a sign on our desks saying, "Don't just sit there, do something." If you visit somebody's office and that person is in a meeting or on the telephone, you're hesitant to knock. You don't interrupt a person who looks busy. On the other hand, if he or she is sitting in a pensive state, you don't hesitate to disturb such a colleague—after all, that person is "not doing anything." In order to counter that tendency, perhaps the sign on people's desk ought to say:

Don't just
do
something.
Sit there.

The renowned mythologist and teacher, Joseph Campbell, used to tell his students, "Follow your bliss." He explained that when people commit to their own deepest instincts toward happiness, they enter an adventure zone where doors of possibility and deep fulfillment open to them—sometimes seemingly miraculously. Campbell was aware of the tremendous danger posed by stress in these times; that our organizations' pursuit of the almighty dollar can use people up and burn them out. As an antidote, Campbell prescribed having what he called a "sacred space," a time or place where each day you can go and momentarily forget about the day's duties and all the crises reported in the newspapers. There for a few moments, you can calm down and get in touch with your purpose. Decisions can be made, and a calm state of mind achieved, that will impact the way you act upon returning to the day's tasks and demands.

A forward-looking organization, recognizing the universal need to recapture meaning through solitude, could institute the "sacred space" for itself and for its people. Perhaps this would take the form of an actual physical space in the building; perhaps it would mean a 15-minute employee discretionary time out each day. Such a policy would say to employees that the organization recognizes everyone's need for daily renewal. Out of this sacred space, new ideas and dimensions of improvement and growth would surely emerge.

Conflicting Advice

To many of you, this advice flies in the face of logic. For years now, you have been told repeatedly by management gurus and practitioners alike that the one best way to raise productivity (and hence, shareholder value) is to downsize, de-layer, and divest yourself back to better health. Accepting this to be true, it has become second nature for today's business leaders to carve rather than improve or create. They find it much easier to raise productivity today by slashing assets and headcount than they do by growing sales through raving fan efforts or tomorrow through the creation and exploitation of new competitive space. Hence, the current obsession with downsizing, reengineering, and outsourcing.

Attractive as this shortcut to asset productivity may appear at first blush, the reality is, it has seldom delivered the desired results. And the evidence for this is mounting. For example, the April 20, 1996 issue of the *Economist* reported that, "A recent survey by the American Management Association (AMA) found that *fewer than half of those companies that had downsized since 1990 went on to report higher operating profits in the years following the move; even fewer say improved productivity*."

Thus, though de-layering, downsizing, and divesting can correct mistakes of the past, they do little to improve the company today or prepare it for the markets of tomorrow. Which brings us back to our initial argument: if you want to stay competitive today or get to the future first, you must be willing to tolerate some organizational slack *(time and space for people to think)*, and be prepared to lessen your fixation on short-term financial performance.

To drive the point home, take a moment and reflect on how much time your people spend *thinking* rather than *doing*. If the vast majority of their time is spent doing rather than thinking, how will they ever find the time to improve what you are doing now or to uncover and experiment with new business opportunities and anticipate changing customer needs in preparation for tomorrow?

Taking this question to the next level of detail, think what you would do if, in the course of reengineering a core business process, you discovered that 10% of the people involved in that process were redundant. Would you:

- Stay the same; make no changes
- Fire them all, thereby removing any slack in the system
- Fire a small percentage, if any at all, thereby leaving each person with some "free (discretionary) time" to further the efforts of either a P or an F Team.

If you accept that simply getting smaller doesn't have much residual value, *and* if you accept that continuous improvement and innovation will be the basis of competition in today's markets as well as tomorrow's, the answer to this question should be obvious.

In the strategic model for change we are proposing in this book, leaders must not only support but encourage quiet thinking time. When leaders ask everyone to use his or her discretionary time either to improve the present or develop the future, they are implying two important things. First, that everyone should have some built-in discretionary thinking time as part of his or her daily work routine. Second, that there will be some specific managerial directives on how best to use this time. Unless leaders are proactive about creating downtime, it will never happen. The rule for managing creatively in constant whitewater is to create strategic "eddies" in the work flow where none presently exist.

PRAISE

Nothing motivates people more than recognition. We have been emphasizing that catching people doing something right brings out their magnificence. In the same way, if we are to release our **own** magnificence, we must catch **ourselves** doing something right. When was the last time you caught yourself doing something right? Unless you're unusual, you find it hard to praise yourself. Most of us catch ourselves doing something wrong, and criticize ourselves for it. No wonder we have a hard time recognizing our own magnificence!

Catching yourself doing something right is a matter of managing your self-talk. As Norman Vincent Peale proved time and time again in his classic book **The Power of Positive Thinking**, positive self-talk will outstrip negative self-talk every time. To catch yourself doing something right, first decide what you want to be doing. You do this by articulating your mission and values.

Your personal mission and accompanying values make up your life purpose. By purpose we mean your reason for being—something toward which you are always striving. A purpose is different from a goal in that it has no beginning or end in time. It is ongoing. Having a clear purpose gives meaning and definition to life. Some people act as if making money is their purpose; they put all their energy into accumulating cash and assets. But purpose can never be about achievement; it is much bigger. While making money is a goal we can strive for, it's not a big enough purpose. Purpose has to do with one's calling—deciding what business you are in, as a person.

Having a clear purpose makes it easier to accept the gift of your own magnificence and to continue to believe it. So let's look now at the building blocks of a purpose statement. In order to know your purpose, begin by looking at what you already love to do. What you love to do, what opens your heart in a deep and satisfying way, is probably exactly what you ought to be doing. For example, you might love teaching so your purpose in life could be "to be a loving teacher of simple truths."

PERSONAL MISSION QUESTIONS

- Why am I in the world?

- What is my overarching purpose?

- What would I like to be said of me after I'm gone?

- What difference is it going to have made that I was here?

PERSONAL VALUES QUESTIONS

- What is really important to me?

- What do I stand for?

- What three values do I want to live by?

- Which of those is most important?

Once you know what business you are really in, you are able to monitor yourself on a day-to-day basis and begin to notice certain actions that are more in line with your purpose than others. One way to do this is through journal writing. Keeping a journal that monitors yesterday's triumphs sets you up for self-praise. What did you do yesterday that makes you feel proud? What did you do that brought out the magnificence in someone else?

When you are learning something new (like catching yourself doing something right) or unlearning a past unwanted behavior (like negative self-talk), you must not wait until you do it exactly right to give yourself a praising. **Exactly right** behavior is made up of a series of **approximately right** behaviors. So be kind to yourself and cultivate the habit of self-praise, by noticing your almost-right behaviors and celebrating the fact that they indicate that you are going in the right direction. Those of us with the habit of negative self-talk—focusing on our mistakes— need to find a way of gathering and sending forces in the other direction. Keeping a journal is an excellent way to remember who we really are. When we can locate and maintain contact with the center of peace within us—our calling—whatever is going on in the world around us will have less effect.

Since this embracing of what is best in us and for us represents the exact opposite of the denial that keeps us forever self-critical and sad, often the question becomes, "How do I come to experience this acceptance?" Mostly it's a mindset—thinking more about the good you do than the bad, recognizing that for the most part you really do spend more time lighting candles than cursing the darkness. Whenever you find yourself beginning to have self-doubt, remember there's nothing you need do to earn your way into acceptance and magnificence. It is your birthright; just claim it.

CONTINUOUS PERSONAL IMPROVEMENT

Once you have committed yourself to the adventure of remembering who you really are, you have begun the most important journey of your life. To remain on the path you must make up your mind that, regardless of the changes going on around you, you are going to control your circumstances by means of **continuous personal improvement**. This means facing up to the areas where you are weak, and resolving to work on yourself daily to build inner strength. That strength is built in two ways.

1. By learning to say "No" to limiting habits and attachments that rule your life and bring you only negative results.
2. By identifying your gifts and strengths, developing them, and using them in the service of others.

By these means you will learn that true peace and harmony are not to be found "on the outside," in the world of business, family, or other pursuits or relationships. Finding that you **can** upgrade your own attitudes and behavior, you will be introduced to the calmness that no outside influence can touch. You will know the truth that:

197

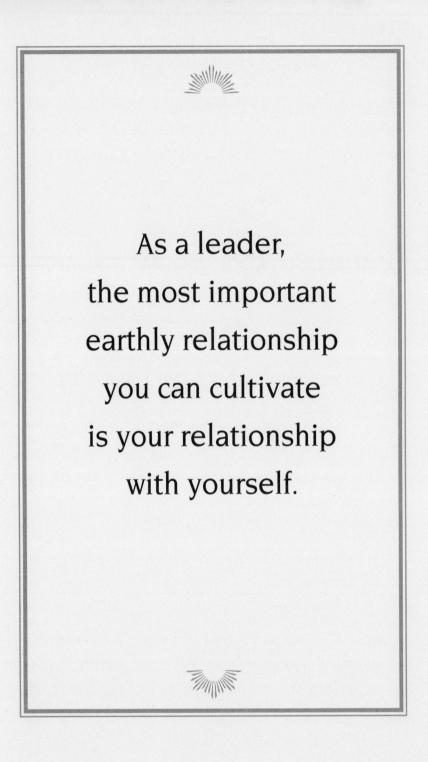

As a leader,
the most important
earthly relationship
you can cultivate
is your relationship
with yourself.

The Purpose Of Organizations

For most leaders, the process of keeping their ego under better control will require some form of daily inner-fitness regimen: journal keeping, contemplation, prayer, and so on. Once they have such a program under way, they are ready to look at work through a different set of eyeglasses. In fact, in order to be truly world-class, everyone in an organization must develop a different perspective on work altogether. They must acknowledge that the organization's primary purpose is not to make money, but to provide service (profit is the applause you get for satisfying customer needs and creating a fulfilling work environment).

Organizations continue to struggle with the seeming contradiction of providing service and making money. After all, service costs. The point is, it's not one or the other. Business that doesn't make a profit is either philanthropy or a hobby. Business that doesn't fulfill a need is a scam. When service (fulfilling a need) is emphasized, and appropriate attention is also paid to costs and profit margins, people in the organization can transform their attitudes toward their tasks ("I am helping people through my work"). In so doing they open the way for personal growth, for at work you produce something, but in service you **become** something. That's what we mean when we say that the real work of the world-class organization is service. In a way, it's an entirely new definition of the real purpose of an organization; at the same time, it's age-old. The twenty-first-century organization **can** exist for all, not just for itself or its shareholders. By the way it fosters relationships within the company, the organization can serve the spiritual needs of its employees. It's possible for employees to think of work as the place where they are nourished and renewed in mind, body, heart, and soul. The organization can contribute to the spiritual well-being of all who work within it in specific ways that produce loyalty and commitment as payoffs.

An organization that not only articulates but acts out an ethical mission and set of values can be a place where people experience safety and security. Provided that people feel they are treated with dignity and respect, and that mutual integrity is at the heart of every interaction, a spirit of unconditional safety reigns within the organization. Even if it must downsize, it will do it in a way that protects and provides for people. It comes from an entirely different place.

FINAL THOUGHTS

Everyone must take responsibility for understanding the concerns that they and other people have about change, and they must also be willing to ask for what they need and be there for others in their time of need. We hope we have done that for you. If there is an on-going implementation theme to this book, it is the one on the next page.

Effective change
is not something
you do to people.

It's something
you do with them.

The stress of operating in two dimensions—trying to improve the present while working on the future—makes absolutely essential the development of calmness and inner peace in the leader. The ability to remain calm amidst all this stress and strain is an important trait of effective leaders. They can ride the roller coaster of doing business today, and at the same time not be dramatically affected by the ups and downs of life. By paying attention and learning to control their *in*-vironment, they are able to be effective amidst a changing *en*vi-ronment. Where does this calmness come from? It comes from within.

These leaders are happy with who they are and what they do. They've found the resources within themselves to be at peace. As a consequence they're not dependent on external conditions—money, recognition, power, etc. This is especially critical in a time of seemingly chaotic change when it's rarely possible to find and maintain peace from outside sources.

Do you feel good about yourself? Are you at peace with yourself? If not, how do you find that peace?

The need for calmness and inner peace is not limited to leaders but makes itself felt throughout organizations whenever effective partnership with employees is sought after.

We have repeatedly suggested in this book that people in organizations need to take the time to think. The irony of this is not lost on us for in these hectic days of continuous change, it seems as if the last thing leaders can afford to do is free up people's time. But we say that if you want to be truly world-class, the first thing you have to understand is that *you have no conception—not even the faintest inkling—of how great your organization could be, once its people's cumulative brain power has been freed and focused*. This release of "corporate magnificence" is the result of a shift in perspective that occurs at all levels of the organization. If Einstein was correct, our problem is not what we see, but what we see *with*. We who stand at the brink of the twenty-first century can't see where the path leads because we're using twentieth-century glasses with which to gaze at it. At the very least we need radical solutions, and the only way to find them is to get "outside of our box."

Finally, if you are going to live in an organization that is constantly changing and improving its present while at the same time designing its future, you can't be possessive about anything, or put your self-esteem up for grabs on a day-to-day basis. Creating world-class organizations is all about contributing to the success of the journey and helping others to do the same. "World-class" begins in the leader's own soul. That gets us back to the title of this last chapter:. "Do I Have What It Takes to Live in a Two-Curve World?" We think so. Do you?

WHAT IS CLASS?

Class never runs scared. It is sure-footed and confident in the knowledge that you can meet life head-on and handle whatever comes along. Jacob had it. Esau didn't. Symbolically, we can look to Jacob's wrestling match with the angel. Those who have class have wrestled with their own personal "angel" and won a victory that marks them thereafter.

Class never makes excuses. It takes its lumps and learns from past mistakes. Class is considerate of others. It knows that good manners are nothing more than a series of petty sacrifices. Class bespeaks an aristocracy that has nothing to do with ancestors or money. The most affluent blue blood can be totally without class while the descendant of a Welsh miner may ooze class from every pore.

Class never tries to build itself up by tearing others down. Class is already up and need not strive to look better by making others look worse. Class can "walk with kings and keep its virtue, and talk with crowds and keep the common touch." Everyone is comfortable with the person who has class—because he is comfortable with himself.

If you have class, you don't need much of anything else. If you don't have it, no matter what else you have—it doesn't make much difference.

Howard E. Ferguson,
author of **The Edge**

REFERENCES AND BIBLIOGRAPHY

Each reference is listed in the order it appeared in each section of the book.

INTRODUCTION

- The opening quote in the Introduction came from Nicholas Imparto and Oren Harari, **Jumping the Curve**. San Francisco: Jossey-Bass, 1995, p. 28.

- Dunlap, Al. "The Business World According to Al Dunlap." January 1996 issue of Delta Airlines Inflight Magazine **Sky**, p. 68.

- The source of the F. Scott Fitzgerald quote is not known.

- The Steve Case quote was taken from an article written by Tom McGrath, "Talking with Steve Case." **US Air Magazine**, March 1996, Volume 3, Number 3, p. 14.

CHAPTER ONE *Once Upon a Sandcastle: Building Tomorrow Today*

• The Marvin Weisbord quotes were taken from his book *Productive Workplaces: Organizing and Managing for Dignity, Meaning and Community*. San Francisco: Jossey-Bass Publishers, 1987.

• Technically the tendency of the human brain to fasten upon relevant data and connect it to its object of desire is known as *reticular activation*. For more information about reticular activation see Newman, James W., *Release Your Brakes!* Studio City, CA: The PACE Organization, 1995.

• Charles Handy's comments about the Sigmoid Curve were taken from his book *The Empty Raincoat*. London: Hutchinson, 1994, pp. 50–51 and 55. See also Handy, Charles, *Beyond Certainty*. London: Random House (UK) Limited, 1995.

• Block, Peter. *Stewardship*. San Francisco: Berrett-Koehler, Publishers, 1993.

• Howe, W. Stewart. *Corporate Strategy*. New York: Macmillan, 1986.

• Stratford Sherman's comments about change appeared on page 25 in the article "A Master Class in Radical Change," December 13, 1993 issue of *Fortune* magazine.

CHAPTER TWO *Redesigning the Castle: First-Curve Improvements*

• The Jon Madonna quote was taken from Imparto and Harari, *Jumping the Curve*.

- The model describing the elements of an organization developed by Mary Gelinas and Roger James is contained in *Collaborative Organization Design—Consultant Guide*. Oakland, CA: Gelinas-James, Inc., 1993. Peters, Waterman, and Philips made a similar descriptive attempt with their "7-S Framework." See their article "Structure Is Not Organization," *Business Horizons*, June 1980.

- Blanchard, Kenneth and Michael O'Connor. *Managing By Values*. Escondido, CA: Blanchard Training and Development, Inc., 1995. This book will be revised and republished by Berrett-Koehler Publishers in January 1997.

- Treacy, Michael and Frederik D. Wiersema. *The Discipline of Market Leaders*. Reading, MA: Addison-Wesley Publishing Co., 1995.

- Percy Barnevik (ABB's CEO and president) quote came from Sumantra Ghoshil and Christopher A. Bartlett, "Changing the Role of Top Management: Beyond Structure to Processes," *Harvard Business Review*, January-February, 1995, p. 86.

- Blanchard, Kenneth, John P. Carlos, and Alan Randolph. *Empowerment Takes More Than A Minute*. San Francisco: Berrett-Koehler Publishers, 1996.

- Blanchard, Kenneth and Robert L. Lorber. *Putting the One Minute Manager to Work*. New York: Wm. Morrow and Co., Inc., 1984.

- For more information on Rick Tate's work see Heil, Gary, Tom

Parker, and Rick Tate. *Leadership and the Customer Revolution*, New York: Van Nostrand Reinhold, 1995.

• Blanchard, Kenneth and Spencer Johnson. *The One Minute Manager*. New York: Wm. Morrow and Co., Inc., 1982.

• Nelson, Bob. *1001 Ways to Reward Employees*. New York: Workman Publishing, 1994.

• Hamel, Gary and C. K. Prahalad discuss "operational competencies" in their book *Competing For the Future*. Boston: Harvard Business School Press, 1993. The core competency examples were taken from C.K. Prahalad and Gary Hamel, "The Core Competence of the Corporation," *Harvard Business Review*, May-June 1990, pp. 80–84.

• If you want to find out more about leadership style and its impact on culture, a study of Situational Leadership® II would be helpful. Ken Blanchard originally developed Situational Leadership® with Paul Hersey. It gained prominence in 1969 in their classic text *Management of Organizational Behavior*, now in its 7th edition (Englewood Cliffs: New Jersey: Prentice Hall, 1996). After finding that some critical aspects of the original model were not being validated in practice, Blanchard created Situational Leadership® II based on the thinking and research done by colleagues Don Carew, Eunice Parisi-Carew, Fred Finch, Patricia and Drea Zigarmi, Margie Blanchard, and Laurie Hawkins, as well as feedback from thousands of users. For a complete discussion of Situational Leadership® II, read *Leadership and the One Minute*

Manager by Blanchard, Zigarmi, and Zigarmi, New York: Wm. Morrow & Co., 1985.

• Blanchard, Kenneth and Sheldon Bowles. *Raving Fans: Satisfied Customers Just Aren't Good Enough*. New York: Wm. Morrow and Co., Inc., 1993.

• Belasco, James A. and Ralph C. Stayer. *Flight of the Buffalo*. New York: Warner Books, Inc., 1993. See also Stayer, Ralph. "How I Learned to Let My Workers Lead," *Harvard Business Review*, November-December, 1990.

• The cover story for the June 1995 issue of *Inc.* was devoted to open-book management. This report was adapted from John Case's *Open-Book Management: The Coming Business Revolution*. New York: Harper Business, 1995.

• For information on Ichak Adizes' work, write Adizes Institute, Inc., 820 Moraga Drive, Bel Air, Los Angeles, CA 90049. Telephone: (310) 471-9677

• Shula, Don and Ken Blanchard. *Everyone's A Coach*. New York: Harper Business and Zondervan Publishing House, 1995.

• The Jack Welch quote comes from an article in the December 13, 1993 edition of *Fortune* titled "A Master Class in Radical Change," written by Stratford Sherman.

CHAPTER THREE   *Taking the High Ground: Second-Curve Innovations*

• The source of the Bob Galvin quote is unknown.

- Shaw, George Bernard. *Man and Superman*. Baltimore: Penguin Books, 1952.

- To better understand Steve Jobs, read Young, Jeffrey S. *Steve Jobs: The Journey is the Reward*. Glenview, IL: Scott, Foresman and Co., 1988.

- For further information on the relationship between Sculley and Jobs at Apple, see Sculley, John. *Odyssey: Pepsi to Apple—A Journey of Adventure, Ideas, and the Future*. New York: Harper & Row, 1987.

- The Gary Hamel and C. K. Prahalad quote is taken from their book *Competing for the Future*, p. 76.

- Drucker, Peter F. *Post Capitalist Society*. New York: Harper Business, 1994, p. 1.

- Naisbitt, John. *Global Paradox*. London: Nicholas Brealey, 1995, pp. 42–43.

- Gates, Bill. *The Road Ahead*. New York: Viking, 1995.

- The rainfall example first appeared in Pierre Wack's article "Scenarios: Uncharted Waters Ahead," *Harvard Business Review*, September-October, 1985, p. 77.

- Arrie P. DeGeus is the former head of planning for the Royal Dutch/Shell group of companies and is considered by many to be the father of scenario planning. See his article "Planning as Learning," *Harvard Business Review*, March-April, 1988.

- Paul J. H. Shoemacher originated the mountain metaphor in his article, "Scenario Planning: A Tool for Strategic Thinking," *Sloan Management Review*, Winter, 1995.

- Rosanos, Nancy. *Intuition Workout: A Practical Guide to Discovering and Developing Your Inner Knowing*. Boulder Creek, Calif.: Asian Publishing, 1991.

- The Lao-Tzu and Rainer Maria Rilke quotes came from *The Secrets of Joy*. Philadelphia: Running Press, 1995.

- Hamel, Gary and C. K. Prahalad discuss core competencies and the difficulty of disentangling them from services and products in their book *Competing For the Future*. pp. 224–225.

- The Rosabeth Moss Kanter quote was taken from her article "Collaborative Advantage: The Art of Alliances," *Harvard Business Review*, July-August 1994, pp. 98–99. See also her book *World Class: Thriving Locally in the Global Economy*. New York: Simon & Schuster, 1995.

- Bleeke, Joel and David Ernest. "Is Your Strategic Alliance Really a Sale?," *Harvard Business Review*, January-February 1995, p. 97.

- Hamel and Prahalad discuss "expeditionary marketing" in their book *Competing for the Future*, pp. 237–246.

- Blanchard, Kenneth and Spencer Johnson. *The One Minute Manager*. New York: Wm. Morrow and Co., Inc., 1982.

CHAPTER FOUR   *Putting the Right People on the Right Team with the Right Kind of Support*

• Watson, Thomas S., Jr. **Connecting People**. Washington, D.C.: Nuff Publishing, 1995.

• The most extensive research and writing on the brain has been done by Ned Herrmann. See his book **The Whole Brain Business Book**. New York: McGraw-Hill, 1996.

• For some interesting work on the difference between left brain thinkers and right brain thinkers, see Dorothy Lehmkuhl and Dolores Cotter Lamping, **Organizing for the Creative Person**. New York: Crown Trade Paperbacks, 1993. Their quote is taken from this book.

• For further information on the relationship between Sculley and Jobs at Apple, see John Sculley, **Odyssey: Pepsi to Apple—A Journey of Adventure, Ideas, and the Future**. New York: Harper & Row, 1987.

• Ichak Adizes first published his research on the four roles of management in **How to Solve the Mismanagement Crisis**. Santa Monica: The Adizes Institute, 1979. See also Adizes' **Corporate Life Cycles**. Englewood Cliffs, NJ: Prentice Hall, 1988.

• Long-term Adizes colleague and former partner Gerry Faust worked with us closely on this section of Chapter Four. Permission to use the material in this section was granted to us by Faust through his agreements with Ichak Adizes. See Faust, Gerald W.

212

and Clark Wigley. "World Class Teamwork & the Challenge of Working with Difficult People," in *The Winning Spirit: Achieving Olympic Level Performance in Business and Personal Advancement*. Edited by Robert B. Sommer. Glendale, CA: Griffin Publishing, 1996 and Faust, Gerald W. *Driving to Prime*, audio/workbook series. San Diego: Faust Management Corporation, 1992.

- For more information on the Lyles Seven Step Problem Solving Method see Faust, Gerald W., Richard Lyles, and Will Philips. *The Responsible Manager*. San Diego: Faust Management, 1997.

- The Jack Welch quote comes from an article in the December 13, 1993 edition of *Fortune* written by Stratford Sherman titled "A Master Class in Radical Change."

- Lawrence Bossidy's quote appeared on page 70 of an article entitled "The CEO as Coach: An Interview with Allied Signal's Lawrence A. Bossidy," written by Noel M. Tichy and Ram Charan in the March-April, 1995 issue of the *Harvard Business Review*.

- The Machiavelli quote is taken from the classic book *The Prince*.

CHAPTER FIVE *Do I Have What It Takes to Live in a Two-Curve World?*

- Nelson Mandela's quote was taken from a transcript of his Inaugural address.

• The six stages of concern were adapted from the work of Gene Hall and his colleagues at the University of Texas, at Austin. Their original research was funded through a grant from the U.S. Department of Education. See Hall, G. and Hord, S. *Change in Schools: Facilitating the Process*. State University of N.Y., 1987; Hord, S., et al. *Taking Charge of Change*. Assn. for Supervision and Curriculum Development 1987; Hall, G. and Loucks, S. "Using Teacher Concerns as a Basis for Facilitating and Personalizing Staff Development," *Teachers College Record*, 1979; Loucks-Horsley, S. and Stiegelbauer, S. "Using Knowledge of Change to Guide Staff Development." *Staff Development for Education in the '90s*. Teachers College Press, 1991.

• Drea and Patricia Zigarmi have integrated the stages of concern with Situational Leadership® II to help facilitate organizational change efforts. For more information on Situational Leadership® II and organizational change call Blanchard Training and Development, Inc. at (800) 728-6000 and ask for a preview of the video "The Organization" from the SLII® Video Series.

• The concept of "What you resist persists" was identified by Werner Erhard, founder of E.S.T.

• For an extensive discussion of the human ego, see Blanchard, Ken. *We Are the Beloved*. Grand Rapids, Michigan: Zondervan Publishing House, 1994. See also Nouwen, Henri J. M., *Life of the Beloved*. New York: Crossroad, 1992.

• The HELP model first appeared in Blanchard's *We Are the Beloved*.

214

- The Henry Ward Beecher and G. K. Chesterton quotes came from *The Secrets of Joy*. Philadelphia: Running Press, 1995.

- MacDonald, Gordon. *Ordering Your Private World*. Nashville: Oliver-Nelson, 1985.

- Peale, Norman Vincent. *The Power of Positive Thinking*. New York: Fawcett Crest, 1956.

- For extensive information on self-esteem, listen to Blanchard, Kenneth, and Jennifer James. *Inner Management: The Importance of Self-Esteem* [sound recordings], Escondido, CA: Blanchard Training and Development and Jennifer James, Inc., 1989. See also Jennifer James' newest book *Thinking in the Future Tense: Leadership Skills For a New Age*. New York: Simon and Schuster, 1996.

- Glasser, William. *Positive Addiction*. New York: Harper & Row, 1976.

- Covey, Stephen R. *The Seven Habits of Highly Effective People*. New York: Simon and Schuster, 1990.

- The quote about the American Management Association (AMA) survey came from an article "Fire or Forget?" that appeared in *The Economist*, April 20, 1996.

- The Joseph Campbell reference comes from a PBS video series Campbell made with Bill Moyers.

- The "What is class?" quotation comes from Ferguson, Howard E., *The Edge*. Cleveland: Great Lakes Lithograph Co., 1983.

HOW TO CONTACT
THE AUTHORS

Ken Blanchard and Terry Waghorn are available to speak at conventions and organizations on the *Mission Possible* concepts. In addition, these concepts can be brought to life in your organization and personal life through audiotapes and videotapes. For information on these products and programs, or if you have any questions about *Mission Possible* or about Ken Blanchard or Terry Waghorn's availability, contact:

> Blanchard Training and Development, Inc. (BTD)
> 125 State Place
> Escondido, CA 92029
> (619) 489-5005
> (800) 728-6000
> Attention: Harry Paul or Pete Psichogios

BTD also provides in-depth consultation and seminars in all areas of organizational service and performance.

Terry Waghorn can also be reached at:

Nolan, Norton and Company
Euclideslaan I
3584 BI
Utrecht, The Netherlands
Phone 011-30-2525-844
Fax 011-30-2525-292

World wide web:

http://www.kpmg.com

INDEX

219

ABOUT THE AUTHORS

Ken Blanchard, Chairman of Blanchard Training and Development, Inc., and a visiting lecturer at his alma mater, Cornell University, is one of the most successful business book authors of all time. *The One Minute Manager*, first published in 1982, still appears regularly on best seller lists. Among other best selling books he has co-authored are *Raving Fans, Empowerment Takes More Than a Minute*, and *Management of Organizational Behavior*, a classic textbook now in its 7th edition. He also co-authored *Everyone's A Coach* with NFL coaching legend Don Shula and *The Power of Ethical Management* with Dr. Norman Vincent Peale.

Terry Waghorn is a Senior Fellow of the Nolan, Norton Institute, the business strategy think tank of KPMG. He has been observing and studying organizational transformation efforts throughout the world for almost a decade. He is a Canadian, currently based in Utrecht, the Netherlands.